Having God's Best Marriage

by
Clyde Temple III

Chicago, Illinois

ACKNOWLEDGMENTS

I would first like to bless the Lord God with all that I have because He is worthy to be praised. I want to thank Him for giving me the idea that I could write this book and dedicate it to His Glory. I would like to thank my pastor Kirbyjon H. Caldwell of Windsor Village United Methodist Church for being so supportive. If I only reach a single person and they come to a useful understanding of how to keep God's blessings in their marriage, I would feel that I have done something worthwhile. Finally I want to acknowledge all of the marriages hanging by a thread or a word as well as the marriages that bask in the glory of God. Hold on!! Take the Hand of God and walk with Him and listen to His wise counsel. Allow Him to bless you every minute of your life and find a way to give Him glory.

TABLE OF CONTENTS

FOREWORD

by Senior Pastor Kirbyjon H. Caldwell

You might be surprised to know that my priority as a husband to my wife, Suzette, ranks above that of being a pastor. I believe that when I am a good husband to my wife, faithful to the Word of God and the covenant of marriage, then everything else I do is blessed many times over.

As Christians, you are heirs to every good and perfect gift that comes from above. If you are married, your spouse is one of those perfect gifts. It is God's will and therefore in your best interest to learn how to be a good steward of this and every precious gift that God sends your way. His wish is that you prosper so that He may be glorified in you and in your marriage.

God created marriage. He would not allow something that He created to suffer without wisdom. I don't know where you are in your life right now, but whether you are seeking to restore your marriage, tweak your marriage, or enter into marriage, the Lord has a Word and a way for you. Seek His face, read His Word, and honor His messengers.

I believe that God has used Clyde Temple III, through this book to help and move toward a better understanding of His will for your marriage. My challenge to you as you read this book is to let it serve you, testing it every step of the way against the Word of God. Before you turn to the first chapter, page 1, I encourage you to do three things: 1) pray that you receive a spirit of discernment to enable you to understand the deep things of Christ that are hidden in His Word and in this work, 2) minister to your spouse in spirit and truth using the tools found in this book, and 3) share the Good News of Jesus Christ by sharing this book with others.

May God bless you in your marriage now and evermore. Trust in the Lord with all your heart and lean not on your own understanding. In all your ways acknowledge Him, and He will make your path straight. **(Proverbs 3:5)**

INTRODUCTION

American society is being hit with a barrage of images and multimedia content that is a corrosive agent to the materials that hold marriages and families together. These images include sexually suggestive commercials and programming of all types that promotes the idea that one doesn't have to work and get out of one's comfort zone to accomplish a new goal. This content has also become focused on images that promote the consumption of things that bring little or no substance to life. These things include extravagant homes, jewelry, automobiles, expensive clothing, and many other things that call for the expense of great financial resources but bring no value to life. Many people gain every manner of the best, latest, and greatest things, but in most cases they go home to a place of emptiness with no joy or happiness because something is missing. So when we don't find any joy in things, we then turn to another person in our search for fulfillment.

When we do turn to people for love and fulfillment, in most cases we have no idea of whom to pick and how to go about choosing a mate, and if and when we do manage to pick someone with whom to share our lives, we have no idea of how to relate to them because we are educated by media outlets on what to look for in a mate and how to conduct our relationships. In the course of conducting these relationships we find ourselves applying the world's rules, values, and standards to how we run our homes. In most cases we find that if something we are doing is taking us out of our comfort zone, we abandon our commitment in favor of something easier, quicker, or what we are told is better. The problems occur when we analyze the standard of what is better. We then find that what the world has to offer as "better" is simply the next thing, no matter what that *next* thing happens to be. We find that the world has no standards as to what is better or best for the enrichment of human life; it only offers the next thing and tells you to move on to it right now because being true to a commitment that takes discipline, work, and effort takes too much time.

But I tell you that there is a truly better way to live, a truly better way to choose what to do, and a truly better way to achieve true fulfillment. The definitive way to achieve true fulfillment comes from making a commitment to Jesus Christ by way of establishing a personal relationship with Him and completely submitting to His plan for your life. But your troubles don't end there. In fact this is where the trouble begins. Because when you finally discover Christ, Satan uses what you don't know that you carry over into your new life with Christ to try to destroy your relationship with Him and everyone else you may come into contact with. For this reason we must exercise our faith just as we must exercise our bodies so that both can withstand the challenges of everyday life and resist attacks on our health.

To grow strong in Christ you must be in continuous fellowship at your local church and committed to prayer and studying the Word so that you may know how to maintain your salvation. As you study, you must also gain a relationship with another Christian who is much more advanced in the Word and the principles of Christ so that you may be able to ask and get answers to the questions that may arise. The next item on your list is to become added into a dynamic ministry to which you can contribute something tangible and valuable as a member of the community of Christ. Once you have become active in the church, you must maintain your commitment. Being saved and born again of Christ means that you are now under the protection of Christ, but this does not mean that the enemy does not attack. You still have free will and you may make your own choices.

And speaking of choices, choosing a mate is probably the second most important choice you will ever make, second only to your decision to accept Christ as your Savior. It is through marriage that God teaches children how to live. The children learn how to read, write, solve the most elementary problems, and they learn from their parents how to have successful or unsuccessful relationships and marriages. Most people grow up in families that don't give much thought to the fact that children need direct teaching on how to treat the people in their lives so that they may grow into adulthood with an understanding of how to have adult relationships. Instead we have been in most cases socialized by the media and directed by the world's instruments on what is beautiful, how long to search for it, and what it looks like to be successful. But what the world's systems never have told us is exactly what success truly means. The experience of success is found in allowing God to bless you by way of following His plan for your life. When you are in line with God's plan, you are in the best possible position to be blessed and successful. This means that you recognize a relationship with God wherein you are in prayer, studying how to build your family and ministry so that you may help others and bring them to Christ and abide in fellowship with other believers of Christ. When you serve God in this way, you are in the best possible position to make choices that please God that He may richly bless you.

In America marriages are failing at an estimated rate of 52 percent, meaning that at least one of two marital unions have been broken, ending in divorce as reported by the 2000 U.S. Census. (This data has been under attack because of a probable misinterpretation of the numbers and was reduced to about 42 percent.) If we break the numbers down by race, we find that the trends are troubling for African Americans, and if we further break down these numbers into the group that includes believers in Christ, we find that the church is not immune to this siege on the institution of marriage. We find, as reported in a study by the Barna Research Group that of 3,854 adults interviewed from the 48 continental states, with a margin for error of plus or minus 2 percent, that of these study participants while just 11 percent of all adults who participated in this study were divorced, Christians accounted for approximately 27 percent of the population of subjects interviewed, compared to only 24 percent of other adults.

In plain English this means that Christians have problems with marriage even though they are supposed to be closer to God. Not only that, but we also find that the National Vital Statistics System, a branch of the Center for Disease Control, reports a steady decrease in marriages. This clearly suggests that fewer people are finding that marriage is a good option for their lives. This is indicated in part by an increasing divorce rate as well as a decreasing supply of eligible men in the African American community due to health issues, incarceration, and the adaptation of alternative lifestyles on the part of both men and women that don't include marriage.

Social views on marriage in the African American community are being adversely affected by contemporary trends that damage the value of marriage. Joy Jones tells us in her editorial in the *Washington Post* entitled "Marriage Is for White People" the following: "And no one seems to feel this more than African American women. One told me that with today's changing mores, it's hard to know 'what normal looks like' when it comes to courtship, marriage, and parenthood. Sex, love, and childbearing have become à la carte choices rather than a package deal that comes with marriage. Moreover, in an era of brothers on the 'down low,' the spread of sexually transmitted diseases, and the decline of the stable blue-collar jobs that black men used to hold, linking one's fate to a man makes marriage a risky business for a black woman." While this woman's statement may ring true, we must still consider that these same forces have been pulling at marriages and the perception of marriage from the beginning.

The difference from days of old and the present is that pressure is being applied more effectively today and in different areas of life. Today instead of resisting the temptation to abandon the commitment to family and its core values, more and more people are taking the easy way out, thinking that divorce is a way to start over or that not marrying at all will be an effective method of avoiding a failed marriage. Questions about marriage are beginning to be asked in churches: "What happened to the value of marriage and what can we do to make marriages more successful?" The answer is that we must return to and study the biblical origins of mankind, understand how we were created, and most importantly how in these times we can create the best environment for our marriages to thrive in the face of today's challenges. Then we must learn and apply the principles of Christ to our marriages.

CHAPTER ONE

Overcoming a Lack of Understanding: The Creation of Man and Man's Duty to God

Wisdom is the principal thing. And with all you have gotten, get understanding. (Proverbs 4:7)

What Is Understanding?

In the context of this discussion we have to acquire the tools to build the kind of homes that God wants us to have. When a carpenter builds a house, he or she must have the tools that will allow him to build the best house that can be built according to his skill. But the tools it takes to get the job done are only as good as the carpenter's skill in using them. In this discussion the tools we will use to build families will yield results as good as God wants only if we understand them. To use the tools we need for building strong godly homes we need to understand what these tools are, how to use them, and the advantages of using the tools we have available to us. In this project the building is much more delicate than hammering nails into wood, pouring concrete, and laying tile. Our project is about shaping the lives around us by understanding them, and with that understanding we are able to discover more tools to shape and form the homes that God wants us to have. The text above tells us that we should get godly wisdom, and with all that we have gotten, get understanding. The text goes on to spell out the kind of understanding we need. Understanding as defined by Webster is to gain:

a mental grasp

the power of comprehending; *especially*: the capacity to apprehend general relations of particulars…

the power to make experience intelligible by applying concepts and categories…

Understanding also involves other elements that help us use the tools we need to build better homes. Three other tools include discernment, comprehension, and interpretation.

Discernment includes the following but is not necessarily limited to these:

the quality of being able to grasp and comprehend what is obscure: skill in discerning

implies a searching mind that goes beyond what is obvious or superficial

Simply put, you have to be able to hear the message and be able to make some sense of it. You must also have a useful place in your life to put this message so that your understanding of it makes common sense, unlike some text book presentation from someone talking down to you. But discernment comes from seeing the way it works in your life in a way that helps you to recognize concepts more clearly in the future. Discernment can also be defined as being able to understand or absorb something with little or no instruction. Discernment is when common sense, good sense, knowledge, and your spirit work together to get an answer to a question, the solution to a problem, or the wisdom to move in the right direction. Discernment and the Holy Spirit should be close allies in the lives of believers because the Holy Spirit's ministry uses discernment to get God's point across to many believers.

Comprehension is the second component of understanding that should be carefully attended. It means simply the act or action of grasping with the intellect. For our purposes comprehension is the act of putting obscure elements of learning together and creating a usable instrument. If you can understand something, you can generally use it in some way. The third component of understanding as mentioned in the text is interpretation. The root of this word is interpret, and Webster's defines this as: "...to explain or tell the meaning of or present in understandable terms..." Notice that the three parts of understanding involve discernment, going beyond the obvious, comprehension, which is grasping and putting complicated things together to make them usable in everyday life, and interpretation, which is breaking things down and making them useful. Using the tools of understanding, anyone can build a marriage provided they start in the right place and use the right tools.

Understanding How We Got Here

The beginning of a successful marriage lies in gaining an understanding, first, of who God is, and second, of how He created us and what the role of man is in God's creation, more specifically in our marriages. We can find out how we got here and who made us by reading the Book of Genesis.

In the beginning, the Bible tells us, God fashioned the universe in a way that establishes His complete dominion over all things existing and not existing. He established what creativity and power really mean. He then shaped and formed man with His hands and breathed into man's nostrils a living spirit. The very breath of God made man a living soul. The

3

Book of Genesis goes on to tell about how the first man, Adam, named all of the animals and God affirmed man's decision making by allowing whatever Adam named each animal to remain its name without changing it. God placed man above all of the earth and found pleasure in this. Man was the master of all the earth and was with God Himself. But God saw that Adam was not complete. And His solution was woman.

When a man is single and he has his own place, in many cases that place can be pretty nasty. There may be clothes strewn everywhere, his diet may consist of fast food only or take out only, and the way he organizes his place isn't really what you would call organized at all. Even if this isn't true and the man is neat and clean and his diet is in order, in a real way he still needs something more. His life isn't really all that good, but he is the master of his domain—or so he thinks. What he lacks is a perspective in his life that brings balance and order. Man wasn't made to be alone. That is why God created woman: to make sure that man understands that not only is there power but there is also deep, abiding love. Without this balance there would be no mankind.

Marriages Fail Because of a Lack of Knowledge

The biggest reason why marriages fail is because we simply don't know enough about how we got here in the first place, who made us, how we were made, and how to minister and serve each other accordingly. Marriages fail because couples do not understand the key issues that make God who He is and man who he is, respectively. Too many times people in relationships try to become little gods, and they exert their will and their designs upon a plan and design that was perfect

4

from the beginning because God made it. When we take on god-like characteristics because we don't get our way, we deny God's power in our lives by attempting to take His power and reshape the life that *He* created and *you* live and not the other way around. A lack of understanding, in many cases, is expressed in disobedience to God's will. And you might ask why I say this, and you would be asking a great question.

Remember when you were a child and you decided to do something that your parents told you specifically not to do; it was because you didn't understand that the consequences of your disobedience would actually come to pass, nor did you fully understand what those consequences were. So you would test your parents. When you disobey God, the message to God from you is more insidious because you are telling God that you don't believe Him when He tells you not to sin. The impact of this horror is brought more clearly into view when you take into account the fact that God is both omnipotent and omniscient, and yet you stand in His face and tell Him that in a universe that He designed *you* are master. You are telling God, "I got this!" and the truth is you don't got nothing! So to eliminate sin, we must come to a greater understanding of who God is, what He has done in the past, what He does now, and what He will continue to do in the future.

Discussions with Your Spouse: Questions That Point Us in the Right Direction

What is the most important element of gaining understanding?

What are some of the things I should understand as a husband or wife?

What should I do with this new understanding I have gained?

Who are some of the people who gain from what I learn as a husband or wife?

What did God do when He created woman?

What happened when God saw that Adam was alone?

Who was Adam talking to when he spoke upon first seeing his wife?

When God created woman, what need did He fill in man?

(Husbands) How does your wife meet these needs in your life?

(Wives) What do you observe about your husband when he wonders at the way God made you?

Remember This:

Almighty God created the heavens and the earth and everything in it. He created the male and fellowshipped with him. God looked upon the whole creation, saw the heavens and the earth, and saw that it was good. But He looked at Adam and immediately saw that Adam was alone. He immediately recognized that man alone was not good. At that moment He was compelled to meet man's incompletion with His divine wisdom, and immediately He moved to meet man's need for completion by creating a helper fit to make man change from male to mankind, a whole functional creation that could share in ministry and worship. God is Love and Love meets need without hesitation. Love your spouse.

CHAPTER TWO

Understanding More about God

Who Is God?

The first thing we must understand in our quest to know God is to completely accept the fact that we can never, with our limited human capacity for understanding, have a full and complete grasp of all that God is and can do. This means we must relinquish our vanity by admitting that we cannot know everything. We must give up our power. We have no power that was not given first by God. This is the reason why we must carefully observe all that He has created for us and does for us, things that we wouldn't ordinarily pay attention to. In other words, we must slow down and learn to appreciate His creation and begin to see with our eyes His observable power in the physical realm. When we slow down enough in the physical, or natural, realm, we can ready ourselves for beginning to learn about the spiritual impact of God's creation. **Job 11:7:**

"Can you find out the deep things of God, or can you by searching find out the limits of the Almighty [explore His depths, ascend to His heights, extend to His breadths, and comprehend His infinite perfection]?" That is the question we are asking even now, and the answer is at hand. **Job 11:7**

So far what we know about God is that He is omnipotent, omnipresent, and omniscient. God is all-powerful! So we have to say out loud, "I don't know everything and I don't have all the answers! In fact I only have a couple of answers. And God gave *those* to me."

This means that God can do all things!

God is everywhere at the same time. Let me repeat this carefully: God is in all places at the same time.

And, finally, God knows EVERYTHING!

Because of the nature of God, and this is just me talking, I think, He has a lot of authority to tell us what to do and how to do it and where to do it and how often and…well you get the idea! What we know about and can know about God comes down to this: **John 1:1**

"In the beginning [before all time] was the Word (Christ), and the Word was with God, and the Word was God Himself." (Amplified Bible) On this message from God alone we could meditate for a thousand years and still only scratch the surface of the meaning of the existence and scope of our God. So what are we left with to learn the heart of God? The answer is simple to say but unfathomable to complete. We learn God by understanding more about what He has done, what He does, and what He promises to do. More importantly, we have to understand that *everything* God has done is a blessing to us.

The beginning of a successful marriage and relationship is an improved understanding of God and being completely obedient to Him. The New International Version of the Bible tells it like this: "Now all has been heard; here is the conclusion of the matter: Fear God and keep His Commandments; for this is the whole duty of man." **(Ecclesiastics 12:13, Amplified Bible)**

Last Sunday I heard Pastor Bill Winston, a prominent and anointed teacher and evangelist from the Chicago, Illinois, area, in his weekly broadcast, "The Believers Walk of Faith," tells us that the Commandments of God don't end with what is written. This means that you may read what God tells us in His written Commandments, but once we have a relationship with Him, the Holy Spirit speaks into our hearts that which is right to do. This is the opportunity for our discernment and the Holy Spirit to work together. Some of us see this as common sense, but if you want to put it more accurately, this is spirit sense. As God speaks to us through His word, we begin to lay in our hearts what is right to do based on His word, and to do what you know God wants you to do is also keeping his Commandments. "Your word have I laid up in my heart, that I might not sin against You." **(Psalms 119, NIV)**

The Amplified Version goes further telling it like this: "All has been heard; the end of the matter is: Fear God [revere and worship Him, knowing that He is] and keep His Commandments, for this is the whole of man [the full, original purpose of His creation, the object of God's providence, the root of character, the foundation of all happiness, the adjustment to all inharmonious circumstances and conditions under the sun] and the whole [duty] for every man." (Ecclesiastics 12:13) What do we know now? Well, we know how God created the earth and all that is in and on the earth, and we know who God is, and we have some idea of His power. Most importantly, we know what the whole duty of man is and that is to "...fear God and keep His Commandments..." Based on this idea, we can begin to understand how marriages are to be conducted.

Remember when we talked about understanding: "Wisdom is the principal thing; therefore get wisdom: and with all thy getting, get understanding." **(Proverbs 4:7, King James)**

9

The Amplified Bible gives us an even more thorough transmission of the Word. It tells us that the beginning of godly wisdom is to understand.

With every marriage there are two distinct areas of understanding that should be pursued to assure the promise of God's richness. Since we have seen how God created us and that our duty is to obey Him, we must also hear what He has to say about the behavior of husbands and wives. These are His Commandments to us as husbands and wives:

"Wives, be subject [be submissive and adapt yourselves] to your own husbands as [a service] to the Lord." **(Ephesians 5:22)**; "As the church is subject to Christ, so let wives also be subject in everything to their husbands." **(Ephesians 5:24)**; "Husbands, love your wives, as Christ loved the church and gave Himself up for her." **(Ephesians 5:25)**

Before I go any further, I want to bless you with something you really need to prepare for learning something more about how to be a better person in your marriage. I don't want to take for granted an important thing that should be said. If one will learn and understand, one must first fix one's heart to listen. I pray that I have your attention now that you may be blessed.

Remember This:

God created both man and woman, making complete mankind. He holds in His hand all power to make changes to His creation, but when He made all of His creation, He made no mistakes. So it is *we* who should learn how He made us in His universe for us to live in, and when our needs are not being met by our partner, we should communicate with Him that He may show us how we may correct our errors that leave our spouses' needs unmet. We must also completely submit to His power and trust Him to be God. We must realize that if we trust Him, we can live in victory. We must love our spouses, submit to God's authority, and obey His Commandments that our marriages remain within His will and under His protection. Remember what God asked his servant (**Job 31:4-7**): "Where were you when I laid the foundation of the earth? Declare to Me, if you have and know understanding. Who determined the measures of the earth, if you know? Or who stretched the measuring line upon it? Upon what were the foundations of it fastened, or who laid its cornerstone when the morning stars sang together and all the sons of God shouted for joy?" God is all powerful and has great plans to prosper you.

CHAPTER THREE

Man and Woman:
Understanding Each Other and How God Made Us

Now that you are listening and we understand some things about God, His nature, and His Commandments to us, let's see how He intends husband and wife to live, love, worship, and serve. It's really important to marriage that each partner in this union desires to be a blessing to their spouse. To be a blessing we must understand how God placed us in His plan. To understand this, we must first understand the nature of our partners and ourselves. We go back to Genesis to find this out.

Genesis 2:15-17 tells us that God formed man from the dust and created everything in man's environment to sustain him. From this we can gain some key insight into how God created the human male and female. We see from the scripture that in their original form, that is, without outside interference and influence, man and woman were made and placed in an environment that was safe and free from death, disease, conflict, hunger, thirst, or any lack. God created the male first. That is significant because even in the beginning God knew that man needed to learn from his origins how he should behave and what his purpose was.

Genesis II tells us, "And the Lord God took the man and put him in the Garden of Eden to tend and guard and keep it. And the Lord God commanded the man, saying, You may freely eat of every tree of the garden; but of the tree of the knowledge of good and evil and blessing and calamity you shall not eat, for in the day that you eat of it you shall surely die."

Originally man had a simple life free of all the trappings of modern times, but he was alone. He had only a single commandment and a job: not to eat of the tree of knowledge of good and evil and to tend the garden, and he was told clearly the consequences of any disobedience. In this state the human male had but a single voice that he would hear and recognize as the One true Authority; and the voice was that of God Himself.

At that time the devil couldn't fool Adam because he had no one to use to fool him. Satan hates man in communion or communication with God alone, but what he hates more is man and his wife worshipping God, so he wages war on the relationship of man to God by attacking God's precious creation, man. He does this by the use of false reasoning and confusion. But at this point in creation Adam was alone. He had all the animals to keep him company, but they were vastly insufficient. They were simply not enough for him. God knew that the creation of humanity was not complete and that the human male needed a helper fit to complement his existence on earth, so He completed man by creating woman.

From reading **Genesis II 18-22** we see what God did to create both man and woman. We see that God made mankind in His image. This means that we bear the mark of God, His image, His essence. Because we are made as we are, we must worshipfully minister to each other in all of life. A very important single point is made in the following scripture taken from **Genesis Chapter 2:** "Then the Lord God formed man from the dust of the ground and breathed into his nostrils the breath or spirit of life, and man became a living being." It is significant that God in making man did two things. He first formed man from the dust of the ground, and secondly, He breathed into man the breath of life, which made man a living soul unlike any other creature God had fashioned. So now we know that mankind has been given a spirit, soul, and body by merit of the fact that God himself breathed into man a living soul.

The Male, Natural and Spiritual

There are elements of a man's existence that make him susceptible to the things that happen outside of his spirit, that is, in the natural, physical, or carnal world. This part of man's existence is known commonly as his instincts. Man's instincts constantly wage war against man's spirit, which cannot be corrupted. Immediately after God created the male, He bestowed upon him responsibility and dominion. The dispensation of this authority and responsibility is universal. In other words, God made man responsible for every gift bestowed upon him by God. With authority and dominion come responsibility.

Another way to look at authority is that one may have authority over something, but that authority is maintained only at the disposal, grace, favor, and pleasure of God. So not only do we have dominion, but we also have stewardship. God gave man power over all of the earth and responsibility to take care of it with honor and respect for God.

15

Now there is a constant battle between the natural man, the part of a man that follows only instinct and carnal motivations, and the spiritual man, the part of man that desires to serve God. The natural man clamors for basic things that gratify his flesh and his ego. He desires power and he desires physical gratification. The natural man does not understand that he has already been given these things by God, but the spiritual man understands that if he serves God, all these natural desires will be quenched and there will be no lack when man submits to God the desires of his being by allowing God to bless him rather than to acquire these things of his own accord.

The natural man barely has a mind, but that mind only works to gorge itself with pleasure and carnal gratification. The spiritual man has complete fellowship with all that God offers him. He has a mind that yields to wisdom, he has a heart that worships God, and with those two his body likewise serves God. His speech is directed, his steps are ordered, and his desires are completely fulfilled. The natural or carnal man when confronted with a challenge to his power or the diminishment of his gratification will instinctively attempt to destroy whatever force he perceives either reduces his power, interrupts his gratification, or threatens his existence.

Abraham Maslow created a scholarly model of how God made natural man and placed man's needs in a hierarchy and ordered them as follows:

Body (Physiological) Needs such as air, warmth, food, sleep, stimulation, and activity. This need concerns biological balance and stable equilibrium (homeostasis). These needs can be very strong because if deprived over time, the person will die.

Security (Safety) Needs such as living in a safe area away from threats. This level is more likely to be found in children as they have a greater need to feel safe.

Social (Love and Belongingness) Needs such as the love of family and friends.

Ego (Self-esteem) Needs such as healthy pride; ego needs focus on our need for self-respect and respect from others.

Self-Actualization (Fulfillment) Needs such as purpose, personal growth, and realization of potentials. This is the point at which people become fully functional, acting purely on their own volition and having a healthy personality.

Notice that the first two items on the list of needs seem to exclude other people, but the following three tend to include people to make man a fully functional and healthy creature. So let us imagine man (Adam) in the garden alone, with God watching him. Adam is with the animals on Earth in the garden. He has power and responsibility over all the Earth, but he is alone with no one else like him. He cannot fully appreciate how God made him, and the Book of Genesis doesn't speak at all of any joy Adam may have had alone. He has no one to talk to or spend time with. At this point we can begin to think that the only way that Adam can become fully functional and healthy is to share life with someone other than himself. God saw Adam's condition and acted immediately. **(Genesis 2:18 - 22)**

God created the only solution for man that would make the communion between man and God complete. He created woman out of and for man. God made woman the complete helper for man so that he could achieve the ultimate goal, which

17

is complete submission to God in all that he (man) does. Once man cleaves to his wife and they become one flesh everything makes sense because the marriage relationship is placed first in worship of God and the provision of family need. When Eve was brought to Adam by God, Adam saw God's power to meet every need conceivable. Now the two could become one flesh, worshipping God and serving each other. Adam could then see his own frailty and powerlessness when alone as a man and without God. Adam could see that woman was the part of him that helped him worship God as a whole creation. And understanding that, every time he looked upon the woman, he fell on his knees and worshiped God, thanking God for making him complete and allowing him to serve and love his wife and make a family that worshiped God.

Marriage was the first relationship wherein man and woman came together, realizing the completeness of their union serving God together. God having created both man and woman gave the two the ability to see the power of God. Man could then perceive his wife as beautiful, and woman could perceive her husband as beautiful and appreciate what a blessing God was to them by having created one for the other. After God created man and woman, he freed them to serve and love each other in the confines of His structure: marriage. It is from that structure and model that we can become whole and functional families.

Satan and His Hatred of Families

From the beginning of time, Satan has tried to wage war on God and His whole creation. Satan doesn't want men to realize their power; he doesn't want women to realize their power. He doesn't want either to find happiness, love, fulfillment, or a healthy relationship with God. Satan wants to reduce man and woman to their carnal and instinctive level of living, where man and woman perceive each other as threats. He wants man to beat and abuse his wife and children. He wants women to dishonor their husbands, belittle them, and make them feel as if they were powerless and immature. He wants the children of these marriages to have no leadership, that they may grow out of control in a world poised to exploit them and eventually cause them pain and death. Husbands and wives have the power to make Satan a non-factor in marriages by following in marriage the principles of God. These principles work because God created marriage and He knows how to keep husband and wife safe.

Remember This:

God created man and woman, and in our natural state we are directed to love each other and worship God. Satan hates everything that God created, especially mankind. When God created woman, Satan thought that he would try to destroy this union by confusing them and lying to them and causing them to sin. Satan does not want husbands and wives to see the glory of God, so he lies to us and causes us to treat each other like we were enemies so that he may stop us from serving God. Satan wants to first separate man from woman, then each individual from God so that he may completely destroy us when each is alone. When you confront confusion or challenges, remember against whom you fight. **Ephesians 6:12 (Amplified Bible)** says: "For we are not wrestling with flesh and blood [contending only with physical opponents], but against the despotisms, against the powers, against [the master spirits who are] the world rulers of this present darkness, against the spirit forces of wickedness in the heavenly [supernatural] sphere."

CHAPTER FOUR

Seeing God's Purpose in Picking a Mate:
Are We Getting It Twisted?

Get Yourself Together Before Your Mate Arrives

Carla and Desmond

Carla is 29 years old, has a law degree, an M.B.A., and is articulate, outspoken, warm, and fiercely loyal and protective of those she loves. She comes from a family that saw her father and mother divorce when she was 13 years old; and she had the horror of seeing her mother devastated by the breakup of the marriage. Her mother resented her father and rarely had anything good to say about him. Consequently, Carla became a compulsive, overachieving, workaholic, stopping at nothing to see that she would never have to depend on a man for success, affirmation, or definition.

As a result of her overachievement, Carla succeeded at becoming a fierce financial producer, making $163,000.00 per year in a firm where she will make partner with little or no problems. She expects her mate to make good money and to be able to provide a good living for the family, but the problem is that she makes enough money for two families to live well— and spends as much as she makes on clothes, cars, shoes, jewelry, and travel. She also expects her husband to be a great lover, listener, and father if she decides she wants to have children. She loves to go to the club for happy hour and listen to music and likes that fact that many eligible bachelors go there to unwind. She loves to shop and can go through a thousand dollars a week in shoes alone. She expects her man to support this spending habit, or at least make enough money for her to continue it as he pays the bills.

Desmond is 36 years old, six-foot-three, and weighs about 210 pounds. He has a mustache and goatee, with a bald-shaven head. He played professional football for three years, made all pro, but was injured and his market value went down. He was later released from his team, but he made good on his income by investing aggressively and making adjustments to protect his assets at the right time. He is worth roughly 6.2 million dollars and climbing, and much of his assets are in cash. He is now doing well and runs a marketing firm and a sports representation agency. Desmond expects his mate to be attractive, glamorous, dignified, extremely sensual, and fit. She should also have a keen desire to please him. She must also be able to cook and be a great mother to his two children as well as the ones they will have together. He is quite frugal until it comes to his two daughters, whom he dotes on because they miss their mother who died of an overdose of heroine and cocaine. He was never married to their mother and tried to help her get clean, but the temptation was too great and her commitment to be sober was too small.

Both Carla and Desmond want their mates to have attributes that they think are attractive, but in reality they have no clue as to what they need from their mates or what will make for a successful relationship and marriage. Not only that, but each of these individuals has behavior patterns that could cause great harm to the establishment and maintenance of a relationship. People have to make a commitment to lead a life free of the old contaminating things that caused them to mistrust and doubt so that they can see another person in the way God wants them to be seen. When we can place money and appearance in their proper place, people become much more valuable and their character and spirit finally come into focus. The point is that no matter how we look or how much money we have, we must look beyond what we can see so that when we choose someone to share our lives with, we do so knowing that there is work to do—and it may not be all that pretty.

Andrea and Paul

But what about people who just try to make it and barely have enough to survive? Well let's look at Andrea and Paul. Andrea is 31 and has a four-year-old son. She is high school educated and works as an accounts payable clerk in a small company. She wants to be married but she is waiting on God for a husband. She goes out to dance every once in a while, leaving her son with her parents. She has a great relationship with her parents, but they only stay together because they cannot afford to live apart. But Andrea has never known this. All she knows is what she sees. She sees her mother regularly disrespect her father, while her father hopelessly lumbers through life. Her mother forgets the fact that Andrea is learning from her how to have a marriage just like her parents'. She has no other usable example. Andrea wants a husband like her father who has always been a good provider and to her has exhibited strength and steadiness in his decision making, even though he has been known to be rigid even when he is wrong. She wants a provider who will love her son as his own and will take good care of her so that she can feel secure and safe. Does she really know what security is?

Paul is 33 and just last month was released from prison after having been tried and convicted of possession of a controlled substance with intent to distribute. He has been in prison for ten years. He has nothing and no hope for a future because he has no skills that are current with today's demands. He does have a very supportive family that is committed to see to it that he gets a good start. Paul has three children who have not seen him since he left and are not in his life at all.

The question is which of these people are more likely to have a successful marriage? Think carefully because the answer is not very obvious. The answer is found by discovering what you have that supports your success, what you have that challenges or threatens your success, how to get the most out of what you have going for you, and how to completely remove from your life that which can and will destroy your every effort to become all that you can become. Simply put, everyone in any situation needs to commit to a personal relationship with Jesus Christ that He may bless you with all that He has to offer those who follow Him and keep His Commandments.

Here is what you need to do for yourself on a personal level. You must first be added to the kingdom of God by accepting Jesus Christ as your Savior then standing ready to change your life by putting it in line with His plan for you. Once you have been added to His Kingdom, you may enjoy the power to overcome every possible obstacle that may come against you. After you establish this relationship with Christ, you must get into fellowship with a local church that will nurture your growth in Christ. Then you must look into yourself and let Him show you where you need to be healed and what in your life may challenge the relationships you develop. Finally, you must begin to make the necessary changes immediately. This means getting Christian counseling at a personal level.

My point is that you cannot expect to be able to select a mate and have a successful marriage without first getting your personal life in line with God's will. When you do that it will not matter that you only just got out of prison or that you have three children that you have no idea how to take care of or that you come from a family that is cold and unprotected or that you were molested or that you never knew your father or mother. Your relationship with Christ will provide you with every kind of instrument of victory over any of the things that could challenge you in your walk with God. Beyond that, the Lord also provides you with other Christian people with whom He may bless you so that you may see how He protects and defends us against the enemy and provides us with the weapons to resist the attacks of the enemy. We have to get to a point where we live in victory instead of always feeling as though we were under attack.

In case no one has told you, it is all right to get professional help in your challenges. A Christian therapist is the right way to go for many Christians who need concrete answers and a way to get back onto the path to victory when mental and emotional issues need attention. When you get professional assistance in gaining the proper insights on how to apply the principles of Jesus to your life in preparation for marriage, you will be able to recognize some critical elements that will prepare you in your journey through life with another person.

Things You Want in Marriage

You need to know what you want in a mate, but you must first know yourself and how to recognize your potential mate. This list is a beginning point that will tell you what issues you should cover with a professional (clergy or therapist) who can help you prepare to deal with the rigors of relationships.

You want to have some indication as to what pleases you within the principles of God.

You want to have some idea of what displeases you.

You want to be sure that what pleases you is in agreement with God's plan.

You must know how to communicate effectively what you want and do not want.

You must be able to disengage a relationship that is not godly or healthy before you invest too much of your best resources into it.

You must understand that there are boundaries in every kind of relationship, and these boundaries must be respected and shared or they will not work for either of you.

You must understand how to become sensitive to another person's need to be heard when they speak.

You must be able to ask the right questions when you are not sure you understand so that you may be sure that you comprehend what your partner is trying to tell you.

You must respect the issues to which your partner shows sensitivity and handle these issues and items as if they were your own. If you cannot or refuse to do this, expect to be either alone or in a very one-sided and unhealthy, ungodly, empty relationship.

You must be willing to allow your mate to meet your needs.

You must realize that you are responsible for meeting the needs of your mate, and you must agree on what those needs are.

These items are just a start for what could be some very enlightening times of growth in your own life. You may even find out that you are not ready to marry. Or you may find that you don't know if you are ready to marry. But if you discover that at a personal level you are ready to marry, then it is time for you to seek premarital counseling. You heard correctly: seek premarital counseling before you even set a date or know whom you want to marry. We should seek individual counseling to determine our readiness for marriage because we can never foresee the moment when the person we can love for the rest of our life will arrive or when we will find him or her. We must be prepared at a personal level to deal with our own problems so that we will be able to be a blessing to our prospective mate.

The truth of the matter is that if and when you fall in love, or however your mate enters your life, both of you will have a past life that directs your present behavior. Your job, should you choose to be a good mate, is to examine your life, list the things that could challenge your relationship in marriage, and develop strategies that will assist in the growth of your marriage and deliver you from the issues that could challenge or destroy your marriage. These issues could include Desmond's tendency to spoil his children without teaching them how to earn things in life, or the probable perception of Carla that leads her to believe that if she depends on a man for anything, she would become vulnerable to him and he would exploit her. Or you may be like Paul who has been separated from society because of prison, and you have no idea of what it means to live in today's world, marked for life, separated from opportunity, and therefore unable to meet the demands of marriage. Or maybe you are like Andrea who has an idea of what a family looks like but never really saw or was taught how to deal with the issues that cause married couples simply to coexist instead of living and loving and adjusting to a life that is always changing and demanding growth.

The key is to locate a resource that can assist you in your preparation for becoming the mate that God wants you to be. And you must also be sure that this resource is available whenever you need it. This may mean that you must find a church fellowship that supports your whole life, not just the emotional experience that you tend to crave every Sunday. Churches must provide a ready resource that is not like the fire department that reacts to the fire alarms when it may be too late, but like the doctor when you see him for your annual check up or the technician that services your car before trouble occurs. These resources have to be ready to move into action before there is apparent danger so that if and when there is danger, the challenges will be manageable. Usually, by the time a married couple seeks counseling it is almost too late because by then they are seeking to justify their respective positions instead of really making an honest attempt to expose the challenges they face and responsibly deal with them head-on, committed and in a spirit of victory. You prepare to have a good marriage before you enter into that marriage.

Picking Your Mate with Perspective

A Few Things to Know

Let's say that you have gotten counseling, you are constantly in prayer seeking God's face in how to conduct your personal life, and the most wonderful person you ever met comes into your life, and this person is a real blessing to you. The truth is that you will still find things that you don't like about this person or that you are not really that comfortable with, especially if you are looking for those things. There are several things you need to know about your potential mate before you get caught up in what you think is love. In one of his Sunday morning services Kirbyjon Caldwell, Senior, pastor at Windsor Village United Methodist Church, told us this about love: "Love meets needs." And since this is absolutely true, you must understand what your needs are. And to determine that, you must know and understand how God created you and what He placed into you that you might know what you need and what your mate needs. In today's world there are several stock, or absolutely necessary, attributes that any mate must have to build a godly and blessed family:

Your mate must be good at something that meets your needs so he or she has your respect.

Your mate must be attractive to you so that you look upon him or her with favor and desire.

Your mate must be able to do business honorably and skillfully.

Your mate must be able to fight and win a battle, be it a great battle or a small battle of great consequence.

Your mate must acknowledge a personal and continuous relationship with God as evidenced by his or her acceptance of Jesus Christ as personal savior.

Your mate must have a desire to do what is right in the sight of God.

Your mate must be ready to agree that Jesus Christ will be the head of the home.

When your mate possesses these attributes, there will be no issue in the past or in the present that will challenge you to the point of defeat. No weapon shaped or formed or fashioned against you will be able to succeed in any attempt to cause any harm to your home. If your mate possesses these qualities at the time you meet, you both will know how and where to seek and find the kind of godly assistance you need for your relationship. When these qualities are present, your mate will be good at something in life that can meet a need that your spirit seeks in a mate. Your mate must also be attractive to you because someone you desire to marry must have a quality that you perceive by looking at them that draws you to them so that your physical bond may be complete because man and woman were made to fit together physically as well as spiritually. This is God's will for husband and wife.

Your mate must also be able to conduct personal business in a way that is honorable and skillful because no family needs excessive credit card debt or excessive spending habits that ruin your family's opportunity to be ready to receive the financial blessings that God has waiting for you. If you or your mate have developed habits that cause you to spend all you make as soon as you make it, you are making it harder to get into position to receive the blessings that God intends for

His people to have. The way your mate conducts business will honor both God and your family so that whatever is done in business results in conditions that promote success in the task at hand. This means that you are able to be good stewards in saving your money and giving to the Lord and His purposes as He directs you. This is important because you must handle your home personal finances as you would a business, and you and your mate must have the skills and resources to conduct your personal finances as you would a business enterprise. When God blesses you, you will need these skills to manage what He gives you or you will not be able to keep your wealth.

The ability to fight a great battle or a small battle with great consequences is a quality that speaks to character. Your mate must be able to wage war against the enemies that come against your home. He or she must know when the great battle is at hand as well as the small battle with great consequences. This means that your mate must have enough discipline to remain faithful to doing what is good even in the face of great conflict. And to prepare for this, your mate must be able to get up and go to work every day, make that weekly bank deposit, maintain regular giving to God, as well as simply be faithful in giving that little kiss on the way to work.

The smallest things take discipline because Satan does not want you or your mate to be faithful in any of these things because he doesn't want you to be blessed. The longer one is faithful in a multitude of the smallest of things, the more likely he or she is to be faithful in the greatest battle. Great battles are won in small victories.

Next, your mate must also acknowledge his or her relationship to God by becoming saved and living life as a witness to the life, death, burial, and resurrection of Jesus Christ. This doesn't mean that your mate must be a great preacher or teacher or evangelist, although it would help a whole lot if they were, but it does mean that their behavior is motivated by the fact that they love and acknowledge their commitment to God. So when someone asks why they didn't go off on the coworker who was way out of line, they will say: "I know a better way to live. The Bible says that 'a soft answer turneth away wrath...' and I am committed to trusting God that this is right." Every good thing they do is because of their commitment to Christ, and they aren't afraid to tell anyone. Your mate will always want to do what is right because the Lord is the head of their home.

No matter how much you prepare for a mate and how many wondrous things you see in your mate, you must remember that when you meet you cannot foresee what work your mate will still need to complete in his or her life, and you don't get to pick and choose what that work may be nor can you choose what you want to deal with after you get married. You have to step up and use the tools that God has blessed you with and then learn how to see and enjoy the victory over Satan. What so many people in these times do when they see the first sign of trouble is forget about all the blessings and wonders that God has provided, and instead they focus on the one thing that Satan wants them to see, the thing they don't like, or they only see the big battle instead of how to win that great victory through being faithful in the smallest of tasks every day. God has given you every resource to do battle, that you may see how God works in your life to defeat the enemy. And He has already provided the victory that you may know His joy.

Chapter Five

Keeping God's Commandments:
What Are They, Anyway?

For the Menfolk: "Husbands Love Your Wives..." (Ephesians 5:25, 28)

We have already established that men are an expression of God's power. They tend to demonstrate in their behavior a tendency to engage in conflict: they hunt, overcome physical challenges, and provide things for their families. This is the model for the prototypical man in the beginning, at a time when life was simple and the forces of society were not so encroaching on the lives of people in families. In today's society the enemy attacks the family by fragmenting family life, taking it apart piece by piece and making it harder to transmit and receive clear messages, he makes it harder to get simple tasks completed. When this happens, a complete understanding of events, circumstances, and situations cannot possibly be achieved enough of the time, nor can misunderstandings be avoided.

Another point of attack is the fact that now males and females are having trouble defining a proper division of labor in the family. The world today demands more production than ever. It demands more money, more time, and more attention away from providing important essentials for the family. In American society there has arisen a tendency for males to come under attack by way of a negative perception by women who make more money than their spouses or their potential spouses. Since many people define their power by how much money they make, the perception is that the less money a person makes, the less power they command, and the less power they command, the less respect they deserve due to the fact that they may be a poor financial performer compared to those who make a great deal of money. Too many times we hear this "No romance with no finance…" or we hear "You can't get it for free!…" The fact is, not everything is for sale. So stop selling it or buying it NOW! If that which is priceless is constantly being put on the market for sale, and if people will compromise their relationship to God for money, we have become a people who worship for profit. And money becomes our god. When we worship a god that can be spent, expended, stolen, exchanged, burned, or worked for, where is our salvation? That kind of worship leaves our salvation only here on earth and definitely terminating. When you die, it's gone and never will return to serve you. The key to fulfillment in relationships is to keep God's Commandments and seek His face and approval.

But how do you do that in today's world of pimps, pushers, players, tricks, and hookers? The answer is simple. Men, don't pimp your wives. Do not allow your wives to engage in addictive behavior. Do not teach your children to be used or to use others. Do not leave the arms of your wife to gain comfort or companionship. Do not pay for sexual gratification or allow the sex in your marriage to be some kind of reward only for special occasions, and don't make your wives have to sell their bodies to make ends meet. Be a man of God. Lead them to behavior that sustains and renews the spirit while gaining critical insight into the fact that the fundamentals of life have not changed but the techniques by which we overcome the challenges of today at a physical level have changed, and we must learn to adapt in a godly manner. This means becoming powerful without the assistance of money. This means putting money in its proper place of servitude to humanity. This requires power gleaned from some place other than this Earth. Allow your relationship with God to empower you, and take this power to your marriage.

If you cannot let go of money as a prime source of gratification, get some professional help immediately and pray unceasingly as you go through the process. The best way to have a marriage based on God's power is to start it right in the first place. This begins with you. **James 4:10 (Amplified Bible)** tells us: "Humble yourselves [feel very insignificant] in the presence of the Lord, and He will exalt you [He will lift you up and make your lives significant]." This means that true power, which is one of man's chief desires, is achieved by becoming humble in the presence of God. This is a beginning toward understanding who you are compared to God and allowing God to be Himself in your existence.

Once you as a man humble yourself and allow God to lift you up, you may share this power with your family. The results may not be immediate, but they will be certain. But the time lag does not mean that you simply become inactive and just wait for something to happen. You must wait upon the Lord. **Isaiah 40:31 (King James version)**: "But they that wait upon the Lord shall renew their strength; they shall mount up with wings as eagles; they shall run, and not be weary; and they shall walk, and not faint."

There is a point of controversy in the use of the phrase "wait upon" in the English language. Standard English scholars agree that the use of the phrase "wait upon" means to serve, but its misuse in speech and writing has caused much confusion. In many cases the phrase "wait upon" has meant, to those who misuse it, "wait for" something to happen or someone to arrive rather than to "wait upon" or serve someone. To "wait for" is clearly meant to be used when one wishes to allow the passing of time to prove something or to allow time for an event to happen. In this case the translation is meant to empower, both in the context of the text and in the lives of those who actively serve the Lord. This passage is meant to activate those who serve God to serve actively. The runner does not wait for God to make him or her faster; he or she works out and makes the body strong and fast to prepare for the task of winning the race. Likewise in the passage "they that serve the Lord will be strengthened again." No amount of piety or pomposity will redeem your marriage from the depths of destruction if you do nothing but look holy. You must serve and ask God for holiness, grace, blessing, and favor.

You can't just put up a front and expect that the enemy will not continue to attack your marriage. You can front if you want to and see what you have left after you decide that your fronting is not working. You will have nothing! Your power is made complete through serving the Lord and others. This means your wife. True enough, you lead and have authority over her, but that power is not yours to take; it is yours to receive at the Lord's pleasure and discretion, provided you serve Him. Any power a man has is given to him. Just as any other blessing that God has given to you, if you are not an honorable and proper steward of that gift, you will surely lose it.

Having been awarded power by God is a great thing and a terrible responsibility because you must serve God with your power by blessing others with that power. This job is made simple because of the help that God gave us in His Word. (Remember the Word God tells us about in Ecclesiastics 12:13.) Based on this truth, we must recognize God for who He is and serve (wait upon) Him in everything we do. We must think in service to God; our behavior must be in service to God; and our speech must be in service to God. So marriage is not just being married or putting on some big expensive show for all of your friends and family. That's only a wedding. We must conduct our marriages in an active way, much like a conductor conducts a symphony orchestra. We are free to love our spouses in so many ways, but we must love our spouses deliberately, on purpose, thoughtfully, and very carefully. We must think of ways to uplift them and remind them why they are good for us. **(Proverbs 18:22)** And we must do this without ceasing. Yes, God gave man dominion and power, but this power is to be used in worship and service.

Loving Your Wife

Based on the nature of the male, God has given Commandments that direct him to love and temper his tendency to dominate. We must love our wives as Christ loved the brethren and gave Himself for them. As human beings, we must do this actively and not passively. We must conduct our marriages. We do this by first being mindful of our wives. Secondly, we do this by always speaking to our wives in love. Finally, we must shape and form our behavior so that from two individuals, a single loving creature of God that worships Him and serves Him can be created. We do this by serving each other as we serve God.

Being Mindful of Your Wife (I Think of You in Love)

When we think of our wives, we put our carnal minds in a place where even if we as men are thinking sexually, we are not in a position to sin because we are thinking about our wives. When we think about our wives, we must be mindful of their needs. Not every woman has the same needs, so there is no blueprint or any magic solution to making every woman happy other than searching out what she needs and listening to what she tells you she needs from you. If she will not tell you what she needs and doesn't give you anything to go on, you cannot be expected to read her heart. You must discover what she needs by talking with her about these things and clearly coming to an understanding that you know what she needs. Typically, a good rule of thumb for making sure you understand what she tells you, is to have her say what she needs, then repeat back to her what you thought she said. If she agrees, you are on the right track. In this way you may begin to think of ways to provide what she needs. Remember, what each spouse needs is something they alone cannot provide for themselves.

There may be times when your wife will have no clue as to what she needs, but you must still pray for wisdom and discernment and that God will reveal the right choices for you. What you provide for your wife is what compels her to crave being blessed by you. The security she desires lies in knowing that when no one else remembers or cares or asks, you alone know and remember some special thing. So you cannot afford to be absent minded. You cannot put off the power of your blessing with "I forgot," when subtleties mean so much to her. Your wife's love is something she chooses to give to you, and as you conduct your marriage within God's plan, she begins to develop into a woman who does not want to be without you. She becomes a woman who looks for the next wonderful and kind thing you will do, the next point of light you show her in your imagination, the next moment of encouragement that she doesn't want to come from any other source but you. As you serve her, God gives you power and protection from the enemy.

Speak to Your Wife in Love (I love You with My Words)

Remember that your wife was created as a helper, fit for you, taken out of you so that when you speak to her she responds to your words rather than react to them. So when you say what you say to her, she must have the opportunity to understand what you are saying without reacting in defense or attacking you. This takes work because at face value you are the leader and in some cases you should be able to say what's what and that's that, but in reality that isn't so unless you have conducted your marriage with words and decisions that are godly and have earned your wife's trust by her knowledge and faith that your instructions would never harm her. You words must make her feel secure and not create self doubt or doubt of you or your authority.

When you speak to each other, leave no doubt as to the content or intent of what you are telling her because understanding you is the first step toward achieving a successful communication transaction. In other words, any doubt in communication is enough for the enemy to slip in a little lie that can cause a breech that may harm your relationship. Marriages are destroyed subtly, very methodically and very slowly. A statement said in bad taste, words said in anger, lies, half truths, and non-disclosures are all tools of Satan that erode the fabric that makes the marriage strong. What someone does not know can harm or kill him or her if the reason you fail to disclose is to hide sin or some other kind of indiscretion.

You can't be married and live a double life and expect to get away with it. You live a double life when there is a critical mass of non-disclosures that could really make a difference if your wife knew that you were hiding something. As soon as she finds out what you are hiding and that you intended to hide something through non-disclosure, she will trust you less than she did before she found out about your little closet item.

The best possible policy is found in **James 5:16:** "Confess to one another therefore your faults (your slips, your false steps, your offenses, your sins) and pray [also] for one another, that you may be healed and restored [to a spiritual tone of mind and heart]. The earnest (heartfelt, continued) prayer of a righteous man makes tremendous power available [dynamic in its working]." We must confess our sins that we may not live under the influence or consequences of them. We must confess our sins to God as well as to our spouse, remembering the following from **1 John 1:9:** "If we [freely] admit that we have sinned and confess our sins, He is faithful and just (true to His own nature and promises) and will forgive our sins [dismiss our lawlessness] and [continuously] cleanse us from all unrighteousness [everything not in conformity to His will in purpose, thought, and action]." Remember that God forgives sin, and you must also allow people you have sinned against to forgive you. It may not be the easiest thing to do but it is the right thing to do. Besides, no one ever told you that being a godly man and husband would be easy. The best way to never have to confess anything from long ago is to not let anything go to the point where it becomes a long-ago issue and impacts the trust that should be in your marriage.

So now we know that what you don't tell your wife can harm your marriage, but what protects your marriage is what you do tell your wife. In **Song of Solomon, Chapter 7,** are found the words a husband tells his wife that she should not be able to resist. Here is a single verse to give you some idea of how a man should speak to his wife. Verse 1 is a single juicy morsel of joy for your wife; should you choose to love her with your words:

[Then her companions began noticing and commenting on the attractiveness of her person] How beautiful are your feet in sandals, O queenly maiden! Your rounded limbs are like jeweled chains, the work of a master hand. Your body is like a round goblet in which no mixed wine is wanting. Your abdomen is like a heap of wheat set about with lilies.

As God Himself breathed the breath of life into the nostrils of Adam, so should men speak words of affection and adoration to their wives. The Bible tells us in a great number of passages that the tongue controls the power to give and take life. That power is in man as well as God. You remember in the Book of Genesis the Lord in some cases simply spoke certain elements of creation into existence. And when Jesus was in the garden and desired to eat from the fig tree and found no figs, He cursed the tree and not long after that the tree withered and died. (**Mark 11:13, 20**)

The following are references to the tongue that you should carefully consider and apply to the way you conduct

41

the use of speech. As with any gift from God, so too is your tongue a gift that holds in it great power. Look at each of these passages and see just how much power speech holds:

Proverbs 18:21

Proverbs 12:18

Proverbs 12:19

Proverbs 15:4

James 3:5

James 3:6

James 3:8

Gentlemen, my beloved brothers, your tongue should be a blessing to your wife because it is guided by the spirit and should bring life, encouragement, and edification. But before you speak in love to your wife, you must first be mindful. Your mind must be full of the spirit of love for your wife and when you make the choice to speak that love to her, you yourself may be blessed. So consider carefully that the words that come out of your mouth bring life and encouragement. Even when used in admonishment and reproof the tongue must be used in love. In a great many cases thoughts guide the words we use; so concentrate on what ministers to your home in love so that your power will be complete in the Lord. This practice will deliver with your reproof the definite and complete knowledge that you love the one you are correcting. So even when you are protecting your home by teaching others how to live, you must conduct your speech in a manner that allows God to give you the power you seek as a man of God, and you do that through loving your wife and humbling yourself.

Finally, my beloved brothers, you must be in complete submission to God's will in marriage because you are the high priest of your family as it worships God. When there are problems in your home, you are the authority that God recognizes as the head of your household. You are a steward of all that with which God blesses you. When there are no problems in your home, you must also lead your wife in worship that God continues to richly bless all you do.

How God Made Woman

To understand the construction of the human female we must refer to the Book of Genesis and carefully examine the meaning of what caused God to create woman, what God did to create her, and what He said before, during, and after he created the human female.

"She opens her mouth in skillful and godly Wisdom, and on her tongue is the law of kindness [giving counsel and instruction]." **(Proverbs 31:26, Amplified Bible)**

I had an opportunity to visit Gospel Tabernacle Church of God in Christ in Dallas, Texas, one Sunday and I heard for the first time a minister say this about God's creation that is woman. He said that woman is an expression of God's emotions. And to be specific, woman seems to be a reflection of the completeness of God's love for all mankind. In the complete view of the relationships of mankind woman was made perfect for man, and the two come together to worship God for the perfection of their relationship and His purpose for it. The two become one flesh, and the couple is a whole complete creature of worship and servitude to God and each other. Woman completes God's love for mankind. When man and woman love and serve each other within their purpose, the result is that they return love and worship to God through each other. Once they come together, they are still bound to the same single purpose of man to fear God and keep his Commandments.

But at an individual level, what is the woman's role in a marriage? What is supposed to be in her heart that motivates her to serve her husband in love and honor? Understanding the above-mentioned scripture from the book of Proverbs is key to the function of the wife in marriage. If we examine the verse, it tells of the benefit of the wife's behavior. First it tells that the woman is skillful and godly. This is an indicator that the woman of the house or the wife should be intelligent and well studied at what it takes to be godly. This means that she needs to be into the Word and understand the Word as it applies to her personal relationship with God and her personal relationship with her husband. And should she not understand the Word, she reads diligently and seeks counsel as to what the Word means to her in her marriage and in her life. Going back to **Genesis 2:4-18,** it is related that God created man. Let us read directly from the text; this is also the account of the creation of the heavens and the Earth.

When the Lord God made the Earth and the heavens and no shrub of the field had yet appeared on the Earth and no plant of the field had yet sprung up, for the Lord God had not sent rain on the earth and there was no man to work the ground, but streams came up from the earth and watered the whole surface of the ground. The Lord God formed the man from the dust of the ground and breathed into his nostrils the breath of life, and the man became a living being. Now the Lord God had planted a garden in the east, in Eden; and there he put the man he had formed...

The Lord God took the man and put him in the Garden of Eden to work it and take care of it. And the Lord God commanded the man, "You are free to eat from any tree in the garden; but you must not eat from the tree of the knowledge of good and evil, for when you eat of it you will surely die." The Lord God said, "It is not good for the man to be alone. I will make a helper suitable for him."

In this passage it is important to understand that God made man a certain way to function under a specific set of circumstances that he may thrive. But the creation of man is documented to also make clear a special point that God wants us to understand, and that point is that man was made, created, and placed on this Earth alone and given dominion over the Earth and everything in and on the Earth, but he cannot thrive alone. A man alone is not complete. Mankind is not complete with the existence of men alone on this Earth. God makes this perfectly clear when He says with His own mouth: "Now the Lord God said, It is not good [sufficient, satisfactory] that the man should be alone; I will make him a helper meet [suitable, adapted, complementary] for him." God saw that a man alone was not complete, so He completed mankind perfectly by creating woman.

The woman was the adverb to the man. A man is only a man without a woman. With a woman a man can be manly because the woman makes that distinction. In the English language the adverb is a word that modifies or qualifies a verb that sits alone, plainly and unamplified. We can examine the effect of an adverb in the context of God's creation. When God created the male, he created a man, but when He created a woman, He perfectly completed the man and thus created the whole of mankind. Now the male is complete because he can appreciate God's creation of his kind.

God made woman as an expression of His love and compassion for the whole. But some may ask how this is. The expression of God's love cannot be seen unless it is expressed through His first perceiving a need and then meeting that need perfectly. This is perfectly clear since God created a whole universe, planets, stars, moons, the Earth and everything on it and placed man in charge alone. Then God looked upon the man alone, and He could not say that this was good. He in fact said the opposite. He said that it is not good that man is alone. That is the point where God sees that mankind is not finished and that man needs something more to be complete. So we must come to another point in revelation. This is the most important thing that anyone breathing must understand about God. When God sees man in need, He meets man's need perfectly. He perceives, He makes a choice, and then He creates again. This is His love. His mercies endure forever because He saw that that man was alone and incomplete, and He had compassion and created for man the answer to his problems. God created His best. God created woman. After God created woman, He brought her to Adam. At seeing the woman, Adam immediately began to praise God by acknowledging God's love for him. **Genesis 2:23-25:**

Then Adam said, This [creature] is now bone of my bones and flesh of my flesh; she shall be called Woman because she was taken out of a man. Therefore, a man shall leave his father and his mother and shall become united and cleave to his wife, and they shall become one flesh. And the man and his wife were both naked and were not embarrassed or ashamed in each other's presence.

When Adam opened his mouth saying, "...flesh of my flesh..." he acknowledged that God met his need for completion with perfect action. This means that woman met and dealt with mankind's incomplete state. It means that man is not complete without woman. No matter what some theologians tell you about this, the creation story bears out that this is true because God Himself said that it is not good that a man is alone, and therefore I will make a helper fit for him. And to meet man's need, God brought to him the woman as an expression of His love for him and to alleviate the pain God witnessed Adam bearing in his incomplete state. God saw a need and perfectly met that need, and because we as humans need to learn how to do this for each other, He commands us to love one another and meet each other's needs as He meets our needs.

What He Put Inside Man and Woman

When God made woman, He made her to complete man in ways that would draw man to woman and woman to man in their natural state, as He created them. When a man sees a woman he desires, he is attracted to her for that reason. He is meant to be attracted to a woman because everything a man lacks, a woman was given by God to attract man and complete his existence. The softness of her skin, the scents she wears, the clothing she adorns herself with, her hair, and makeup are attributes of womanhood that God placed inside woman to cause the man to be naturally compelled to be with her for life. Inside woman are the things that teach a man how to be more of a man: compassion, love, kindness, mercy, sympathy, empathy, and a nurturing spirit. Alone a man is destructive, relentless, vengeful, merciless, and without a capacity to comprehend true love, which is the compulsion to meet need by acting against that which causes others to suffer.

Loving someone is not passive as some may think, and love is not only for God to act out perfectly. We as human beings created by God must show God love by meeting the needs of those around us. If this is not done, there is no love. This is how love is made manifest in the lives of fleshly beings. This is how God makes love real in the lives of His children. When you love someone, they can see it and know it. When a husband loves his wife, she never has to ask him if he loves her; she sees this every day. When a wife loves her husband, he should never have to ask her if she loves him; she lives out that love in her ministry to him.

When God created woman and brought her to man, He placed into her being an inherent ability to meet the needs of men, particularly her man. When God made woman, He placed into her what He saw as meeting the needs of a man alone. He placed into woman the ability to see God's mighty power to create. God also placed into woman by merit of His having perceived the needs of man alone, an inherent need to see that a man's needs are met in every way possible, including physically, mentally, emotionally, and spiritually. To further break down this dynamic, let's look at what God saw in creation before He created woman. He first saw all of creation and perceived something. That something that God perceived was the fact that man was alone in all of creation. God also perceived that this man alone was not complete. We know this because when God perceived man alone, He spoke that for all time the record would show that man alone is not complete.

And out of the ground the Lord God formed every [wild] beast and living creature of the field and every bird of the air and brought them to Adam to see what he would call them; and whatever Adam called every living creature, that was its name. And Adam gave names to all the livestock and to the birds of the air and to every [wild] beast of the field; but for Adam there was not found a helper meet [suitable, adapted, complementary] for him.... **Genesis 2:19-20**

Let's analyze what God was doing here. First of all, when God saw that man was alone, He also wanted to leave in the record of creation why He operates the way He does, and thus we find out how we should operate as humans. Now when God saw man, He knew that he was alone, but He placed this into the record of creation so we as humans may know what being alone means to man. Being alone means that a man is not complete, sufficient, or satisfactory. Having said this, God also let us know why this was true when He went on to say that, "I will make a helper meet suitable, adapted, complementary for him." At this point, we understand if we only look that without a helper or complement, a man is not a suitable, complete, or sufficient being. And this condition of insufficiency is so profound that God went on to carefully teach us what kind of helper man needs.

The text goes further to illustrate the point that God made the animals, brought them to Adam, allowed Adam to name them, and confirmed his naming of the animals by allowing whatever Adam named the animals to remain as he named them. It must be taken into account that God was teaching Adam and all who read about him that the helper "fit and suitable" for man was not and is not to be found among the animals.

We can only guess what Adam was thinking as he named the animals. He may have been wondering what was missing, or he may have been feeling a deep sense of loneliness because no one in all of creation was exactly like him. He had no one to talk to except God, and God knew that Adam without a helper fit and suitable was vastly incomplete. Adam had no one to help him complete his sentences, no one to smile at him when he was having a bad day, no one to send him flowers that he may know that someone thinks he is beautiful, no one to see the wonder of the wonder of a new day as God paints the sky with His perfect colors in a sunrise. But most importantly, Adam had no one with whom to share his experience of God. Adam was probably pretty pathetic all by himself.

At seeing Adam in pain and loneliness, God was moved and expressed His love for him by meeting his needs perfectly. And so Adam was put to sleep, a deep sleep in the arms of the Lord while God did his work. And from his side God took a rib and fashioned with His hands and His thoughts Adam's helper and brought her to him.

Notice that at seeing God's perfect expression of love in action, Adam immediately worshipped, acknowledging

God's love by speaking words of praise. It is at this point that mankind was complete because man now had two active parts that could come together and minister to each other and praise and worship God together. They could bless God and God could continue to richly bless them. Adam could tell her about God and how things were before she arrived and how lonely he was without someone just like himself with whom he could share God. And they could love each other.

God made a whole world, a man, the animals, and still wasn't finished. When He saw that man was alone, in His infinite wisdom He fashioned the perfect solution to man's problem, and that was perfect love. Eve is the embodiment of that expression. Eve is God's active expression of love for man. Without Eve man cannot fully know how much God loves him. God demonstrated His power of creation through Adam, and He demonstrated His perfect love through the creation of Eve.

God continues to love us by protecting us and finding ways to keep us close to Him in spite of our rebellion against Him. Now it is man and woman's duty to take care of each other. But it isn't quite that simple because Satan doesn't like anything that God made to thrive, so he lays tricks, traps, and lies for us.

Remember This:

Husbands, it is critical that your wife knows that she is appealing to you. It is important that she understands her total value in your life. She must know that she is a blessing from God that you perceive as a divinely placed component of your life. Not only that, but if you remember that Adam immediately worshipped God when he saw Eve and knew that she was the missing part of his existence, you too will fall and worship God every time you see anything that your wife provides that attunes your life to the way God wants it to be. God wants your attention for bringing this wonder into your life. Fall on your face and worship God for this beautiful creation that He made just for you because He loves you. Remember, woman is God's active expression of love for man. He created her to make mankind complete and able to fully worship Him. Husbands, love your wives, and come together that you may worship God.

CHAPTER SIX

"Women, Be Subject to Your Husbands…"

Submitting Does Not Mean Being a Doormat

"Wives, submit to your husbands as to the Lord. For the husband is the head of the wife as Christ is the head of the church, his body, of which he is the Savior. Now as the church submits to Christ, so also wives should submit to their husbands in everything. Husbands, love your wives, just as Christ loved the church and gave himself up for her to make her holy, cleansing her by the washing with water through the Word, and to present her to Himself as a radiant church, without stain or wrinkle or any other blemish, but holy and blameless. In this same way, husbands ought to love their wives as their own bodies. He who loves his wife loves himself. After all, no one ever hated his own body, but he feeds and cares for it, just as Christ does the church, for we are members of his body. For this reason a man will leave his father and mother and be united to his wife, and the two will become one flesh. This is a profound mystery—but I am talking about Christ and the church. However, each one of you also must love his wife as he loves himself, and the wife must respect her husband." **(Ephesians 5:22-33)**

Dr. Juanita Bynum Weeks said in her sermon "Pride and the Proverbs 31 Woman," included in the multimedia book *Teach Me How to Love You* by Bishop Thomas Weeks, III, "Submission means I find his vision, and I put myself in the position to always keep him on top…."

It seems that the reason for this model is that God made the man to be powerful. He should be in the leadership position in a marriage, but the woman is the one who protects the man from attacks of the enemy when he lies and misleads us. The woman fiercely protects the family through loving her husband and seeing to it that his leadership is pure and that his living is correct that he may not fall. The woman completes her husband's vision and protects it from attack. She loves him and gives him the confidence to attack the forces that come against his efforts to serve God and provide the best possible life that he is able to for his family. And where he may be inadequate, she, the wife, makes him adequate so that the family may be the perfect vessel of worship to God.

In some models the husband is the high priest of the family because of his position of leadership. And because of this position of leadership wives must keep watch over their husbands that they may be blameless in the eyes of God. Many families fail because wives either fail or refuse to serve their families. Since woman was provided as an expression of God's love, she must be just that to her husband. Woman's ability to serve in any and every other capacity depends on her performance as a wife. Performance as a wife should be measured by the standard that God himself set when He observed the needs of man and immediately responded to meet those needs.

Since woman's existence is a direct result of a loving act of God, she is the most important person in her husband's life, with God being the head of both. But the question is, how can women perform their duties as wives if there has been no background teaching to support their role? Since God created woman and introduced woman to man, we should probably look to God for the standards on how to be a wife. We can find the models for marriage for each partner through the Bible in both Testaments. So in this book we simply try to make clear how man and woman were created and introduced to each other and how they should live together according to the Bible. Further, we contrast some elements of life on the streets with how God wants our homes to be managed. Now it's time to get real.

A wife in good standing with God in the home has the benefit of a clear eye that sees her husband and all that God wants for him and all that he can be for God and the family. But before she becomes this wonderful wife, she needs to get the trash from the world's view of relationships out of her eyes and out of the home that she establishes with her husband. The world wants women to believe that men are brutes who want only to dominate and reduce their wives' identities and value to nothing in favor of a society that exploits women without acknowledging their worth and recognizing how God created them in the first place. The world wants you to believe that all men want from you is sex, and to a very small extent this is accurate, but sex in its proper place in the covenant of marriage is acceptable to God. The world wants women to believe that their bodies belong to them alone; this is not true. Before you are married, your body belongs exclusively to God, but after you are married, your bodies (husbands' and wives') belong to God within the covenant of marriage and all of its responsibilities.

So no matter if you are married or not, sex is not an option. Sex is for the married and loving. The unmarried should be learning how to become spouses who can do their best in marriage, and the married should be loving each other exclusively, completely, and unconditionally. So, ladies, married or not you do not have a choice as to what you can or cannot do with your body. God determines that. And He has not made a mystery of finding out what to do. The world wants you to believe that in marriage you are supposed to stand up for your rights against your husband, but God wants you to know that husbands and wives decide together how they will love each other in their marriages. In some things men should be able to make definitive choices and not have them challenged by their wives because when these challenges occur, Satan has a way of controlling a marriage; and when he can control a marriage, he can destroy it and neither partner knows what hit them if they are not vigilant and ready to meet the challenges of everyday life in marriage.

The last thing Satan wants to see is a man and a woman having a successful marriage and relationship. How do we know this? We know this because marriage is the first thing God created that Satan attacked. Satan wants to see husbands and wives at odds, fighting and in constant conflict. So be you a husband or a wife, if you find yourself always fighting or annoyed by your mate, you are being used by Satan against God's plan and design for mankind. Before I go any further, I need to give you a word on being used by Satan. There are several characteristics of being used by Satan in any aspect of life that will keep you in bondage to his schemes until everything you ever wanted is destroyed. I need to leave this word with you so that you may apply it and not allow Satan to gain a foothold in your relationships or your life in general. I will number these characteristics as I name them:

Satan is using you if you can never find satisfaction with the things God has given you to keep or conserve. Clue: If you are given a gift and the first thing you think about is the thing you really wanted instead of appreciating the blessing right in front of you, you are being used by Satan.

Satan is using you if every time your mate tells you anything you immediately perceive it as an attack on your person and your reaction is to lash out or react in defense of your position or your behavior.

You are being used by Satan if you spend more time on the job than you do ministering to your family. The more time Satan has with your family, the less net utility you will gain from working on two or three jobs. Learn to take care of what you have, and learn what is truly precious. The impact of leaving Satan with your family has an unfathomable and terrible impact on the family. A generation of latchkey children are at this moment being molested, killed, or otherwise exploited. Parents come home, having spent most of their energy at some job to get things that never satisfy them, and their homes are falling apart. Yet they have no idea why this is happening. They wonder why their daughters come home with babies and why their sons are in trouble with the law, making bad grades or unable to read, or why their children are never home. If the leaders are not seeking first the kingdom of God, their focus will be on things that will never give them blessing, satisfaction, or peace. When this happens, people tend to reach out in a desperate search for fulfillment that never ends, and they tend to latch on to whatever provides them with instant gratification. But they forget that it takes as much time to get things right as it took on all those jobs they work to pay off the bills they overspent to create. You have to spend time with God at His feet and with your family.

If you believe that sex in your marriage is a reward instead of a way of life, you are being used by Satan. Sex in marriage is an expression of love. This misunderstanding happens so much in so-called Christian marriages that many men in these marriages either have affairs or, because they don't want to cultivate a relationship with another woman, they engage prostitutes and find that those sexual relationships are more gratifying than the one they are supposed to have at home. This behavior results in a terrible confusion that leads to an addiction to the gratification they get from prostitutes and relationships they cannot get at home. Many wives in these marriages have nerve enough to wonder what they did wrong. What they did wrong was fail to take care of their homes, and this neglect left a gaping avenue for Satan to tempt, tantalize, and take their husbands away. Some of these women say that another woman took their man, while the truth is they gave him away by either failing to take care of business or, as some do, simply by refusing to take care of her home.

When it comes down to it, a woman's desire is for her home to be the best it can be, but if her time and best energy is not spent in homemaking, she will not have a home to take care of.

Summing up what God put into each of you, male and female, man and woman, husband and wife, is not an easy task, but some insight into what God did when He created us can be gained by examining two major premises. The first is that when God created man, He expressed His power. Therefore, man is a personification of God's power. He made a whole world and created man and breathed into this man His very breath gave man a living spirit. Then God gave the man power over the Earth—the land and the sea. After God did this, He observed the man and perceived him in need because a man alone is not complete no matter how much power and dominion he may have.

Secondly, God responded to the need of this pathetic, solitary man by loving him. God had compassion for this man and did not want to see His beloved creation in pain. So He put this man into a deep sleep so that he would not feel being opened up, having his rib removed, and the rib being fashioned into a woman. But when he woke up, man saw woman and immediately knew that this was the relief to his pain and the completion of his being. Woman is the personification of God's love. Since God is love **(1 John 4:8),** we can see that every time God perceives a need He makes a choice and moves. Therefore, we must act like God concerning the gifts He has given us. We must actively love each other.

Remember This:

Wives, you are God's love for man made flesh. Your very existence makes man whole. God put Adam to sleep that he might not feel the pain of his loneliness as He opened Adam's side and took the rib that He fashioned into a woman. A helper fit for him. Woman, you are the living instrument of God's love and His desire to see that mankind becomes everything that it can become. You must always be a reason why your husband worships God faithfully, and you must worship God with your husband. There are five things that I recommend that you do to make your relationship with your husband more complete.

Pray that you understand your husband's needs

Each time you understand any need your husband has you must immediately act to meet his need so that he may find yet another reason to bless you and worship and praise God for providing him with you.

Every day find new value in what submission truly means so that you may understand that submission is not bondage but is a part of your covenant with your husband and God. (Submission is mutual in nature and function.)

Every day find new ways to come together in agreement with your husband to reach the desires of your collective heart.

See yourself as a helper fit for him and present yourself before God and your husband as that helper. Find ways to become that fit helper.

When you have done these things, your husband should bear witness that you are that helper fit for him. This may not happen immediately in every case, and it may not happen automatically in every case. Finally, be faithful in these practices, remembering that this is a part of your ministry and worship.

CHAPTER SEVEN

Love, Submission, and the Godly Marriage

There are Bible examples that illustrate how we should acquire mates and behave ourselves in marriage, but many people these days abandon the word of God as the final authority on living and even more simply don't want any rules to live by so that they may make their own rules and just live the way they desire without structure or grounding in godly principles. Believe it or not, most marriages, including Christian marriages, are conducted this way and that would account for the staggering rate at which marriages fail.

It seems that when the world says if it doesn't work correctly right now, dispose of it immediately without exercising discipline, compassion, kindness, respect, patience, or good common sense. That is easy for someone in the world's system who wants to discard someone; but when they themselves are on the business end of being disposed of, all eyes get turned to God. But then it may be too late because if you build your marriage on the sand of worldly principles instead of the bedrock of godly principles, it is bound to fail unless you repent and turn your marriage over to God. For many people turning their marriages over to God is too hard because, if you let church folk tell it, you deprive yourself of everything you enjoy. But turning your marriage over to God is actually achieving freedom from all these elements that would have been successful at challenging your marriage. With a marriage based on godly principles, health and prosperity are yours. Remembering our whole duty, which is "…fearing God and keeping His Commandments…," we can look at people from the Bible and see exactly how to conduct marriages.

Proverbs 18:22 tells us that, "When a man finds a wife he finds a good thing." When he finds a wife, he meets with God's expression of love to meet his needs as a man. When love goes well, marriages are blissful havens of generosity, affection, and richness. One such marriage is the one between Solomon and the Shulammite bride. The reason why Solomon enjoyed his wife so much was because he obeyed God's Commandments and loved his wife. And for us today the same standard holds true. So remembering that fearing God and keeping His Commandments is the whole duty of man, we need to know exactly what the Commandments of God are regarding marriages today.

We know from our earlier discussion that in **Ephesians 5:25-28,** God commands us: "Husbands, love your wives, as Christ loved the church and gave Himself up for her…." And it goes further to say, "Even so husbands should love their wives as their own bodies. He who loves his own wife loves himself." This is a major and very dynamic concept that must be examined to understand the kind of love God wants husbands to show to their wives. Many Bible scholars kind of brush over these two verses to enumerate the Commandments as a way of whipping a man into shape, but this word from God is not only directive but it is also a spiritual instrument that directs a man's attention to the kind of love that Christ has for the church and uses it as a model for spiritual composition, meaning spiritual makeup or decorum.

Looking at Verse 25, we see in the language that husbands should love their wives in the way that Christ loved the church and gave Himself for it. This establishes a parallel between husbands and wives and Jesus and the church and sets that standard for how and what men should do for, to, and with their wives. Another important point that is absolutely necessary to understand is that both relationships are holy, sacred, and spiritual in both origin and nature. There is but one difference between the two relationships and that is a difference that should make it easier for a husband to love his wife. God allowed us to feel all of the physical and emotional sensations associated with the love that we have for our spouses.

Another important similarity between these relationships is the fact that in order to redeem us from sin, Jesus was sent to become a living sacrifice that made Him our high priest and whomever accepts Him on His terms shall not perish but shall have eternal life with Him. Our way to God and eternal life is through Jesus Christ, and as a husband your relationship with your wife is to be as holy and as spiritual because the husband becomes the high priest of his family so that through him his family may know Christ and be blessed with the peace and prosperity that God promised those who keep the covenant.

Yet another aspect of the marriage of a husband and a wife is stated in Verse 28 of the text: "Even so husbands should love their wives as their own bodies. He who loves his own wife loves himself." This is a poignant and powerful directive because in a man's natural state he wants power, and he does whatever he needs to do to achieve whatever it is that he desires. But husband and wife, although created separately, were meant to become one flesh, and the selfishness with which a man loves himself and cares for himself is the same love that he lives out in his relationship with his wife. What makes him fulfilled should fulfill his wife. A man's knowledge of what makes his wife feel secure should give a husband great peace because "…he who loves his wife loves himself."

More importantly, when husbands and wives serve each other, they are serving God because God Himself created and anointed this relationship and called it to be the way it should be. Husbands, loving your wives is a ministry both spiritually and physically. It is a spiritual relationship between physically created creatures, a spiritual relationship that bears fruit in emotional, physical, and spiritual forms all at the same time. She is flesh of your flesh and literally bone of your bone, and you as husbands must know this intimately, as Adam knew this instinctively when God brought Eve to him.

Another commandment that God issued is to wives and is found in **Ephesians 5:21-24** "Be subject to one another out of reverence for Christ [the Messiah, the Anointed One]. Wives, be subject [be submissive and adapt yourselves] to your own husbands as [a service] to the Lord. For the husband is head of the wife as Christ is the Head of the church, Himself the Savior of [His] body. As the church is subject to Christ, so let wives also be subject in everything to their husbands."

So many women in this rebellious society have so many problems with this passage that it has caused some breaches in communication and relationships between men and women for quite some time. But that is to be expected because Satan wants us to be confused and at odds with each other, especially with issues related to this passage of scripture. I included Verse 21 for impact purposes to reinforce the fact that what some think this passage means is totally different from what others think, which is that this passage relegates women to a submissive role based on an erroneous presumption that husbands are directed and anointed to be tyrants who have no need to serve or love their wives and families. Placed into context, these commandments work together for perfect peace in a Christian home.

Bearing in mind that husbands are to love their wives as the scripture says—and as God loved man by creating woman out of man—it would be inconsistent with all that God commands for us to anoint a tyrant as a head of household. To further analyze this commandment, remember that God has dictated no commandment that is meant to be simply read and followed blindly without learning what adapting to God's will means to your life. With this in mind, when you hear "...be subject to one another out of reverence for Christ," how can it be thought to mean that God wants you to be dominated by someone other than Him?

We can then turn this statement backward and look at it in a different way by saying out of reverence for Christ, be subject to one another. Notice that this commandment is positioned before the one that instructs wives to be in subjection to their husbands. This is significant because it sets up a hierarchy of submission in the church based on your personal status. It starts by addressing everyone in general, and then it gets specific by addressing those who are married, specifically wives. It then says that wives should be submissive to their husbands, and at the same time it sets up yet another hierarchy, which is between husbands and wives and the Lord. The passage goes on to re assert the parallel between the church and Christ and husband and wife. Since the husband is seen as the head of the house, he is responsible for its spiritual development. Therefore the wife must submit herself spiritually to her husband because, drawing from the parallel, the husband is the high priest of his home insofar as his household worships the Lord.

A perfect example of a husband leading his wife wrongly and the Lord executing judgment based on the order of leadership in the home can be seen in the incident with Ananias and Sapphira in **Acts 5:1-11**. This couple agreed to sell a vineyard, and they reported to the apostles that they would give all of the proceeds to the Lord. But they decided together to keep back some of the proceeds while reporting that they had sold the land for less than they actually had received. Ananias appeared first to report the sale of the land, the profit, and to deliver the proceeds from the sale. He reported that he and his wife had sold the land for one amount, but they had actually sold the land for more than the amount they reported. Ananias was asked if he told the truth about the sale and elected to lie; immediately he was struck dead. Three hours later, his wife showed up with the same story and suffered the same fate. This supports the idea that in the eyes of God husbands will suffer punishment for treachery but if wives agree and conspire in this treachery, they too will suffer because they did nothing to keep their husband from sin. The order of the punishment is husband first, then wife. The husband, Ananias, knew what was right and so did his wife, but he led her wrongly, and because she agreed and participated willingly without repenting, they both suffered the same fate.

This is a stark example of the husband and wife's hierarchical relationship. In the beginning how did Eve find out things about God when she didn't ask Him directly? Who did she ask about God? She had to ask Adam. And Adam told her things about God when they were alone in the Garden of Eden with God, without challenge and before Satan laid siege to their relationship with his deceptions. Anyone outside of a marriage should not be advising couples unless they represent God and are directing them in godly ways. The wife should consult her husband first in any issue of importance, especially issues that have spiritual impact. To sum it all up, we should submit ourselves one to another that we may assist each other in living a Christ-centered life, but in marriages wives have their husbands as the first source of instruction and reproof. There is nothing worse than third-party advice interfering with a marriage and making things worse. This is one reason why husbands are the heads of their households. Another example of the fact the God looks to husbands first in leadership is in **Genesis 3.**

This is a very important chapter, and in one passage we find that Eve was separated from the Word of God, was beguiled, sinned, and then influenced the fall of her husband. The key question here is whom did God address first when He arrived on the scene? He first addressed Adam and not Eve. This tells us that He sees husbands as having the first responsibility for their households.

But there is a model that we should consider that is already given much attention but in different ways, and that is the woman in **Proverbs 31.** We all know the woman described by Solomon. We know her attributes, we know her characteristics, we know what her husband says about her, and what her children say about her. We even know what the community at large says about this godly woman. But my question to you is, Do you think that this woman that Solomon speaks of is fictional or imagined? By no means is she fictional!

This is the other side of the woman Solomon expressed his love for in **Song of Solomon.** All of the aspects of womanhood are included in a virtuous woman, including her sexuality as well as her aesthetic beauty. All things about the virtuous woman, both perceptible and imperceptible, are a part of who she is to both her husband and God. Each of the traits, elements, and attributes the virtuous woman encompasses are gifts from God that should be conducted, maintained, and nurtured.

Many accounts of **Proverbs 31** do not focus on the whole chapter but rather on the virtuous woman of which the mother of King Lemuel teaches. Contextually in Proverbs we find three separate women. We first find that there is a reference to the origins of the teaching, which came from the king's mother who herself must have been virtuous because she understood the value of the virtuous woman and the impact of this teaching on her son's rule as king and man. The second woman is the one to avoid because that woman can bring kings to their ruin. And finally she imparts to him a word on the woman of virtue. But more importantly and subtly, we must also be aware that this model was originally taught to the leader and king, although this passage has become a standard for teaching women the attributes of virtue in womanhood.

We find in the passage that first the mother teaches her son about the loose woman. She teaches him that the loose woman saps him of his strength, and that he should not lose his way among those women who cause kings ruin and destruction. Here we find that husbands need mothers who can teach them well about the causes of ruin as well as how to find the virtuous woman who can cause them to prosper. Thus a man can compare what is virtuous and what is not virtuous in women. We all know what the passage says, but it is also important to know that both the virtuous woman and the loose woman can have an affect on a king as well as an ordinary man. A loose woman can ruin a king in a vast kingdom as well as a simple man in a single home on a single lot in a trailer park. But a virtuous woman is able to make a simple household like a kingdom, a small kingdom into a vast kingdom, and a large kingdom into a great royal empire.

I hope that everyone who reads this begins to understand the value of a woman who does her best to follow God's plan for womanhood and marriage. Throughout the Bible, God has left us with models of behavior and verbal commandments to follow in order to keep us under the protection of His plan that we be may continue to be blessed by Him.

So we now know several important things about what man and woman are to do for God. We know that we are to first gain understanding. We know that our whole duty is to fear God and keep His Commandments. And we know that husbands are to love their wives as Christ loved the church and gave Himself up for it, and that wives are to submit themselves to their husbands as unto the Lord. Hopefully, we understand how man and woman were created and have some insight as to why God made us this way so that we may serve each other better through Him and serve Him through each other.

Academically all of that analysis is good and fine, but the trouble with Bible theology is that people live in the streets and in their homes and on their jobs and not in the church house, where the pastor and church leadership can see us and know how our lives may be corrected. And some of us are fooling ourselves by going to church and hearing the scripture and mouthing the words, and we feel that what the pastoral staff says can only be mastered by those who are securely based in the Lord. Or we hear the excuse that "well, I don't know the Word like they do…," but that is a sorry way to send ourselves to hell for being lazy and irresponsible to God. It is far better to do what He commands us to do and to understand His Word.

"How long, O simple ones [open to evil], will you love being simple? And the scoffers delight in scoffing and [self-confident] fools hate knowledge?" **(Proverbs 1:22, Amplified Bible)**

Satan keeps us from the promises of God by intimidating us and lying to us, telling us that living godly lives is too hard or too complicated or that you just can't understand how to live godly lives, or there are so many rules, and you can't live a perfect life. And some of us look at the church and can only see scandal and dishonesty, which has nothing to do with one's family and its walk with God. The key to living a godly life is in understanding everything you need little by little because you cannot possibly understand everything all at once. So you learn one thing at a time, and your walk with the Lord is one step at a time. The mystery is in how you take those steps in the place where you live every day.

In the next chapter we will look at some ways you can practice making your marriage the way God intended it to be, but before we do that, it is important to understand a simple three-step approach to correcting unhealthy behavior in marriage and recognizing problems so you can end them before they destroy your home. We begin by understanding why God called us to obey His Commandments. Most of the time when we even think about Commandments, we automatically think about constraints and rules because we only see the Commandments without considering how following them impacts our lives every day.

Each commandment that God issues, either written, spoken, or relayed directly, increases freedom, life, and love or redirects behavior that increases freedom, life, and love. So when we see the verse "fear God and keep His Commandments," let's do a simple exercise and replace the words "keep His Commandments" with the phrase "enjoy life, love, and freedom." The verse would then read, "Fear God and enjoy life, love, and freedom; for this is the whole duty of man." Now how difficult can enjoying life, love, and freedom be? Fearing God and keeping His commands can only mean that you will enjoy life, love, and freedom from sin, shame, and death. But again, taking this to the streets and living this way is not simple because it requires placing His Words into your heart and living by them. **(Psalms 119:11)** This requires both husbands and wives to study the Bible to find out how to live and to take each thing they learn and apply it faithfully to their lives. But doing that can be a great challenge if you don't know where to begin.

Remember This:

The Bible tells us that the husband is the head of the house, and this is affirmed over and over again throughout the Bible, with God and man entering into covenants where the husband makes a covenant with God that if kept causes great prosperity for his family and if not is the cause of great pain and trial. We only know that this is the way God decided to set things up. It's not some trick that men played on women to keep them down, and it's not really a great advantage for men because of the dire consequences a man must suffer if he is not a good steward of his home. Ours is not to question God in why He made things this way but how to make His plan the center of our life.

CHAPTER EIGHT

The Beginning of Complete Victory in Your Marriage

Steps to Victory

There are several steps that need to be followed to achieve strong, godly, successful marriages. The data from the United States Census tells us the divorce rate is 50 percent in White America and 68 percent in Black America. Statistically, marriages have an unacceptable rate of failure. This failure rate is attributed to many things such as money problems, too much time away from the family on the part of the couple, affairs, and everybody's favorite, "irreconcilable differences." While the reasons people list in surveys as to why they divorce cite problems that are fundamental, it is obvious that marriages are not entered into in most cases with the thought and the equipment needed to deal with the onslaught of challenges the couple will have to face. Very few of these marriages are truly based on the principles of God or with the way God made us or what His Commandments for husbands and wives mean individually. Hopefully, at this point we understand how God created us and what the whole duty of man is, namely, to fear God and keep His Commandments. It's also very important to know what God says about divorce.

"And did not God make [you and your wife] one [flesh]? Did not One make you and preserve your spirit alive? And why [did God make you] one? Because He sought a godly offspring [from your union]. Therefore take heed to yourselves, and let no one deal treacherously and be faithless to the wife of his youth.

"For the Lord, the God of Israel, says: 'I hate divorce and marital separation and him who covers his garment [his wife] with violence. Therefore keep a watch upon your spirit [that it may be controlled by My Spirit], that you deal not treacherously and faithlessly [with your marriage mate].'" **(Malachi 2:15-17, Amplified Bible)**

Here the prophet Malachi tells us God's feelings about divorce. He makes it plain by telling us that God hates divorce because He made man and woman for each other to be one flesh. The union between man and woman is a spiritual union completed by the two becoming one flesh. Their lives—spirit, soul, and body—become one that they may minister to each other and worship God as one flesh and spirit. But becoming like that to some is very hard to do since it takes complete commitment and surrender. Now we understand that God does not mean for marriages to dissolve, but we still need to know some thing about how to become one flesh so our marriages can survive or be revived.

In the real world for a marriage to occur two people must first somehow meet, and be it instantly or in the fullness of time be compelled into each other's needs because they were made to do so. So the couple decides to become one and begins to make plans to make their union permanent. As this couple fashioned their wedding, filled with opulence and splendor, bedecked with pearls and diamonds and christened with the tears of an adoring fellowship of friends and family, they made the common mistake that most couples make. They fashioned and crafted a beautiful wedding but failed to pass through the threshold of marriage understanding, which needs to be shaped as carefully as the wedding of their dreams. To make a marriage solid and grounded, certain commitments must be accepted without question. We will start with the husband then complete his commitments with those of the wife.

Since husbands are commanded to "love their wives as Christ loved the church and gave Himself up for it," it is critical to understand what love is in the first place. For man and woman love means to instinctively meet each other's needs without question or hesitation. This also includes a directive on how far to go in acting out love. Love is action that completely meets human need in spirit, soul, and body. The scope of a husband's love for his wife is seen in **John 3:16:** "For God so loved the world that He gave His only begotten Son so that whosoever believeth in him should not perish, but shall have eternal life." Just as God perceived Adam's state of incompletion, so shall a man perceive his wife's need; and as God immediately met man's needs in action, so shall husbands meet the needs of their wives. This is a commandment of God. Loving our wives takes faithful commitment to several concepts:

1. Understand what loving your wife really means.

2. Commit to loving your wife

3. Act on that love

4. Know that love and action are one and the same.

5. Be faithful in your love for your wife.

6. Love no woman but your wife.

7. Know that loving your wife means serving her.

Likewise wives should follow the same principles in their commitment to their husbands.

1. Understand what loving your husband really means.

2. Commit to loving your husband

3. Act on that love

4. Know that love and action are one and the same.

5. Be faithful in your love for your husband.

6. Love no man but your husband.

7. Know that loving your husband means serving him.

Loving each other this way is, in fact, loving yourselves because, after all, you are one flesh. When you become one, then you turn your attention to God. What I listed are the personal and individual commitments that each person must make and maintain before getting married because once married, these commitments will be valuable assets in the protection of the precious union that God has given each of you to keep safe and holy. Once you begin to act on these commitments, you may properly begin a marriage. But once you begin a marriage, you must also know without a doubt that you will be challenged. The degree to which you are committed to being as God wants you to be will determine your power to smooth out the rough spots.

Remember This:

If you are to have a successful marriage, make a conscious effort to manage your marriage. Management involves analysis, planning, making commitments, and execution. In these times married couples must take a businesslike approach to dealing with the issues that face their lives. To implement this approach, her are some suggestions:

1. Identify the main issues that cause the most confusion and conflict in your marriage

2. Write these items in list form in order of impact on your lives and on your marriage.

3. Discuss these items and why they are on your list. You may find out that as you discuss them, some will need to come off the list because the discussion alone may find the key to their solution.

4. In your discussion be certain that you place on the list under each item your feelings related to the item.

5. Determine if your issues are problems

6. Determine the solution to each problem.

7. Determine what resources you have to solve these problems and how to access these resources. Some problems will require professional help to solve.

8. Get moving on implementing the solutions.

9. Measure your progress periodically.

10. Get back to work.

When a problem is solved, replace that item on the list with another one. Your work is never done.

Every day businesses face challenges that require professional help to solve; otherwise they would fail in business. Marriages must employ the same techniques to survive. Finally, and most importantly, you must be in constant prayer to ensure that your goals for harmony in your marriage are met.

CHAPTER NINE

Marriage in This Time and in These Streets

The Challenges of Today and Some Ways to Overcome Them

In this day and age mankind has not changed at all. We still have the same needs, and God's provision for those needs have not changed. Woman is still a man's fit helper, and it remains true that when a man finds a wife, he still finds a good thing. There is, however, a big difference between people who are married and those who just have marriages. Those who are merely married have completed a transaction that culminates in a merger of assets and common living arrangements, and sometimes not even a merger of assets, especially money.

For those of you who enter into marriage thinking that you can live as you did before you were married, grow up, stop fooling yourselves, and get a life. Marriage means more than just living together and sleeping together. Marriage means that a man has found the helper fit for him. He has found what God meant for him to have. And his commitment to this one woman is the last the he will ever make and keep. When two such people come together in any age or time in human history, their marriage is a union of spirit soul and body that is committed and consecrated to God by their oath and covenant to each other and to God. This covenant means that they will seek God's face to meet whatever challenges may lurk and use what He has given them together to defeat the enemy.

Satan is still roaming about telling lies in enigmatic subtlety that in many cases goes undetected until the damage to marriages and relationships is both obvious and painful. Those who are just married often don't believe that Satan is telling them lies every day and may even believe the lies that Satan tells them, and these lies in too many cases completely destroy what could have been perfectly good marriages. Now it is time to reveal the three critical areas in which Satan attacks marriages even before they start. And to keep it real, these lies are told in the streets and the damage happens in the streets before a marriage begins, after a marriage covenant is consummated, and even after Satan completely destroys marriages and homes.

Three Perceptual Attacks of Satan

1. *Your Personal Perception of Marriage*

The first area that Satan begins to attack in marriages— even before marriage is consciously considered by the couple— is the individual perception of marriage and how things in a marriage should go. This attack occurs in the home during childhood years, when young people learn what marriage is like, but not necessarily how marriage was designed by God, in the home they grow up in Many times, in a day and age where more and more hours are spent in the workplace at the expense of the development and shaping of the lives of children and family, we become trapped in a society where consumption drives us to work too many hours in the wrong places instead of making the development of our homes our main priority.

The correct order of priorities has been overshadowed by the fact that we get into too much debt buying things we really don't need, and this debt is causing us to spend more hours in the workplace while things at home go largely neglected. When children see this lifestyle, unless they have access to and the benefit of proper direction on how to live responsibly and how to prioritize the development of their homes, they are doomed to repeat this curse of debt and broken homes. Whether their marriages remain intact or if they become another member of the growing hoards of divorced and lost people in our society, these children learn most of what they will know about marriage from their parents in the homes in which they were reared. This is a cycle of learning and behavior that transmits a devastating curse that results in split marriages, poverty, multiple marriages and divorces, physical abuse, emotional abuse and neglect, adultery, fornication, and all manner of failures that destroy the homes and unions that God ordained and anointed and did not intend to be broken and terminated.

The biggest lie that Satan tells is that we know how to conduct a marriage when we have no clue. We only think we love someone enough to have a wedding, but when confronted with marriage, we find ourselves deficient in character, patience, and enough skill to deal with the practical elements of daily life in a marriage. When it comes down to it, your mother and father's marriage should not be your example and model. God's Word is the best example for your marriage, and the reason why it takes time to seek out, locate, and apply godly principles to your marriage is because God wants you to be committed to seeking Him out so that He may be your source of light and direction in defining your marriage and enriching your life. True enough, your parents may have a godly marriage, but you must understand why their marriage worked so you can break the curse of divorce by having an understanding. Also you can teach your children how to be godly people so they may have godly lives and create and maintain Godly marriages.

Your Perception of the Role and Function of Husbands and Wives

The perceptions of the roles of husbands and wives have historically been compared as separate items and historically thought to have been defined by men. Phrases like "a woman's place is in the home," "keep women barefoot and pregnant," and "have dinner on the table when the husband arrives," as well as "husbands are the bread winners" (an indicator that men are inherently supposed to make more money than their wives) are all relics of a long-vanished past and a terribly inaccurate paradigm for gender roles in marriage. Every day you hear so many church people preaching that men are supposed to be the bread winners in the family, when a report from the National Committee on Pay Equity reports that the wages for black women have gained on black men. This would imply that wages among black man and women are being redistributed in favor of black women. That leaves us to infer that wages for black men are either decreasing or their wages are not increasing at the rate at which black women's wages are increasing. This condition viewed through the world's eyes would call for women to seek only husbands who are better providers, but the use of the word provider in this context suggests that being a good, adequate, or better provider means that the more money a man makes regardless of race, the greater his value as a man.

We have so-called Christian people, from common church folk, some anointed with high callings, to the preacher, the deacon, and the elders, preaching and promoting this doctrine of Satan. A man's worth is established by God alone, and no amount of money or status can assert his value to the Almighty God. When people assign or associate another's personal value with anything earthly, they are taking on a role meant only for God. God asserts and assigns human value, and He did this and punctuated how He feels about us when He sacrificed His only Son, Jesus, to die for our sins that we may continue to live. Even now He continues to try and get through to us and we still won't listen. We still pick each other up, and if we shine or entertain or otherwise gratify each other, we then assign value and laud the person. But as soon as the party is over, that person's value is denigrated to nothing, and as his or her usefulness is no longer apparent, he or she is disposed of (divorced). This is what church folk do.

The dogmatic attachment of this church-preached and driven "man is the bread winner" age combined with the current wage trends is causing great tension between black women and men. With the decrease in black men's wages and the increase in black women's, we now find an observable tension between black man and women. This tension is happening because of the competition between the two groups for the same pool of wages. At the same time, women who come from so-called Christian families have adopted this entitlement-minded approach to marriage and their set of qualifications for a suitable mate.

If anyone who reads this book understands nothing else, understand that this approach to marriage is done, dead, never was correct, and is becoming an abomination because it is destroying the possibility for good Christian women to find good Christian husbands because the man does not make enough money! This approach to marriage and finding a mate is not sanctioned by God. I say this on the basis of how God created man and woman and how a man shall leave his father and mother and shall cleave to a wife, and the two shall become one flesh. So women who make six-figures salaries should not exclude the brother who makes only $45 thousand a year or someone who has no degree or someone who only has an M.B.A. instead of a J.D. or the man whose occupation doesn't match their status. Godly people don't get caught up in the world's economic system because God's system is designed to bless you more than any job you work 80 hours a week or six-figure incomes.

The things that God blesses you with are the things that no amount of money can buy. No amount of cash or status can purchase the peace and love of a family blessed by God because they have completely committed to His way and sees each other with love and immediately minister to each other because that is what God does. Having a spouse with compatible physical traits is a good thing, but allowing God to bless a union with atonement is what God means for us to have in this life. Being the bread winner, bringing home the bacon, taking care of business, are all human and non-scriptural concepts that Christian people have gotten too caught up on to see that people are spirit, soul, and body.

In this world women and men in a vain attempt to gain more money and status pair off with others who make the same or more money, have the same kinds of credentials, come from the same socioeconomic background with both parents in the home—and still end up with marriages that are completely artificial and break like crystal at the first sign of a challenge to the character and soul of the marriage. When people today see that something is taking them out of their comfort zones, they immediately dispose of each other. Then they use the same technique to create another losing, ungodly marriage and never once try to find out how God put man and woman together. Nor do they get on their knees to pray that they gain the wisdom to understand and ears to hear His voice that He may guide them into a relationship that He touches with His hand and blesses. I would suggest the following:

1. Stop looking for someone to save you from poverty.

2. You aren't entitled to a man who "takes care" of you.

3. Man was not put here to take care of woman. Woman was created to take care of man so that He may better understand how God loves him and together they may minister and serve God. "I will make a helper fit for him." Time to change your thinking.

4. You don't need a man to take care of you.

5. You aren't powerless or helpless, and you certainly are not a child.

6. Grow up and be whole, woman! Your marriage depends on this.

7. You are a powerful instrument of God, and with the right man you become one powerful example of God's pouring out of His blessings on all mankind.

8. You can only have a good marriage if you surrender your thinking to God and let Him direct your path.

9. Your husband will cleave to you if his heart is right and he wants to be used by God to bless you with his love.

10. You cannot love with words; only love between man and woman was designed to be physical as well as spiritual.

11. If you don't have sex, you don't have a marriage. Stop fooling yourselves about this.

12. Women, no matter how much you can love a man, if he is not fit to be a husband, you shouldn't marry him.

This is not a game. This could affect the lives of many people who are depending on your walk with God to show them how to have a family of their own. Ladies, you may think that I am being hard on you, but this is a time for you to realize that Satan is attacking men and killing them and because of this fewer are available to your vision, but they are still there. Men go to work every day, and some men in our society are undervalued, underpaid, imprisoned, disrespected, unjustly feared, and hated and this is happening at the hands of people who share common origins and heritage.

The Federal Bureau of Prisons reports that African American men comprised 40.1 percent of the federal prison population. Human Rights Watch, an independent non-governmental watchdog agency, reports that state prison populations show that 43.7 percent of the prison population is comprised of African American males. This overall figure is considerably lower than that of several individual states and the District of Columbia, which has an overall population that is 60 percent African American and a prison population that is 92 percent African American. Other states with high African American inmate populations include Louisiana at 62.9 percent, South Carolina at 67.2, North Carolina at 61.1, and Maryland at 72.3 percent. So in the African American community the male population is being threatened, and the size of the group of eligible males for mate selection is diminishing.

We see that along with the consistently decreasing wage earning power, black males who cannot make themselves look productive seem to be targeted for removal from society on many levels. This imbues this group of men with a stain that makes too many look as if there is a whole culture of people who concentrate on entitlement in the face of behavior that is fraught with lawlessness and underachievement. This perception is pervasive not only in majority populations but in the African American community itself in all too many cases.

This multilevel attack by Satan on African American men is causing African American women to reject men who share their culture and experience, and this rejection is reducing rates of marriage in the African American community. It's not that women must now lower their standards; it is that women must now rescue men at risk of being lost forever to the weapons of Satan in his efforts to destroy marriages and families. It is also not that women are encouraged to marry men with criminal backgrounds or history, but to show them that there is hope before it is too late. Women have a unique opportunity to be vessels through which God may redeem good and descent men through their compassion, kindness, and commitment to ministry and worship.

Your Perception of Your Personal Role in Marriage

Satan also separates us and contaminates our thoughts and puts trash into the way we think about our personal roles in marriage. The Bible tells us how to conduct ourselves, but many times we decide to be selfish in the face of what God tells us, and we miss out on His direction and protection. Society tells us to get more money, get the house, get the bigger house, get the bigger house in the trendy neighborhood, get the car, get the degree, get another degree, win that case, go for more, but you never hear the voice of society say be at peace and be blessed. Being blessed is seeking God's will in spite of what material possessions you have. It's not about having what you want but wanting that with which God has blessed you. The selfish soul can never be filled until it is emptied of itself and filled with the Holy Sprit rather than material things.

At a personal level, one cannot achieve materially, academically, and in all other manner of physical ways and expect to keep the rewards without keeping their eyes on God. God didn't make women to be man's maid or concubine, but He made man to rule over the Earth and woman to be a helper fit for maintaining this rule and to be an instrument of God's love for him. Marriage is not about you singularly. That's right, it's not "all about me." It is about two spirits becoming one flesh, and the one flesh functioning as one organism, one physical being with many functions. Each person in the marriage must meet the needs of the other so that the will of God is made manifest in both of you.

God does not want a man to be alone, so he made woman a helper fit. He perceived that man alone was not complete, and His love for man completed this existence with woman being made flesh so that she could show man the love of God. As a woman, if you do not show your husband the love of God manifested in your physical existence as his wife; your fitness as his helper is diminished and your marriage is placed at risk. Any time your marriage gets to be all about you or you decide that your mate should take care of his own affairs because it has become too stressful for you, your marriage is at risk. If you don't help as a wife, you no longer complete his existence and you abandon the purpose God Himself spoke for you, and if husbands don't love their wives and allow their wives to help them, they also put their marriages in jeopardy.

A Word to Men

Some of you will think that I have been hard on women, but this is intentional because the family is under attack. In many cases that's all we hear because no one tells us what is really going on. Many women have been sheltered and the truth is being hidden from them because all we want to see is the large house, the sport utility vehicle, the children, or a life of luxury. It takes a lot more work to make this happen, and it takes everyone working together to make a prosperous life. Men, I have a few suggestions that may help.

Get a job and keep it.

Be a man. This means keeping your word and being responsible.

When you are off work, leave that job where it is. Your family needs you at home enough for you to make a difference. A paycheck is good but it only pays the bills; but a good man at home secures his home.

Remain in prayer.

Don't be afraid to ask for help because you don't know everything.

Be about the business of managing your home deliberately. This means planning to be blessed not just thinking that something will drop out of the sky because you have put in the hours and the dedication on your job.

Gentlemen, you must take care of your families. This means that you must allocate time to render proper attention to ever facet of the business of being a head of house hold. This means that you partner with your wives to create a blessed home that God can bless and protect because you have spent time with God in finding out what it means to have a godly home. Your relationships can only become better with more time invested in them. The old saying still holds true: "If you ignore something long enough, it will go away." This is true of your family. If you as men fail to spend time in your relationships, they will fail and they will be taken from you in very painful ways.

In many cases we find ourselves overwhelmed, and that is not altogether a bad thing because if being overwhelmed results in turning our eyes to God and the bountiful resources He has for us, we will learn that everyone in the home manages their roles with help from God, and this help is gained through a consistent relationship with Him. As a husband, you must take the time to make a home that God will honor with His protection. This does not mean that you will live without challenge. It means that a godly home has a place for its head to occupy and be a conscious manager.

For too long men have gotten a pass and have not been required to do what God requires of you. We are finding that in the African American community men are under attack, but this attack is not taking place as you think. It's not the so-called "man"; this attack comes from a lack of understanding of what it takes to be a man, and how a man meets and successfully negotiates the challenges of today's society. This lack of understanding is causing many black men to face life with a glaring vulnerability and a lack of hope or vision to deal with it.

A young black man makes it clear: "I was with the street life, but now I feel like I've got to get myself together," Mr. Brannon said recently in the row-house flat he shares with his girlfriend and four children. "You get tired of incarceration." Mr. Brannon, 28, said he planned to look for work, perhaps as a mover, and he noted optimistically that he had not been locked up in six months." This article goes further to illustrate that in their younger lives men without the proper skills, combined with a history that causes a perceived predisposition for involvement in criminal activity, are forced into a pattern of behavior that makes them unfit or unavailable for marriage, so women who would otherwise marry them simply don't, and who blames them for not wanting to enter a losing situation from the start. The article went on to talk about private agencies that were attempting to help men of similar circumstances, but never once did it name a single church.

If you can find help nowhere else, you should be able to find help in your church. The article goes on to illustrate something missing in the assistance that private agencies cannot deliver. "The clients readily admit to their own bad choices but say they also fight a pervasive sense of hopelessness. 'It hurts to get that boot in the face all the time,' said Steve Diggs, 34. 'I've had a lot of charges but only a few convictions,' he said of his criminal record. Mr. Diggs is now trying to strike out on his own, developing a party space for rentals, but he needs help with business skills." The church can overcome this terrible lack of hope, but the church must be challenged to meet this need by developing programs that address such situations. And men must avail themselves of these programs to gain critical business skills, character development training, and life skills that help develop a fit, productive, and hopeful man who can serve God and build strong families. It's not enough for these programs to just be available. The church's mission is to seek and save the lost, and most of the time the lost are not that far away, and in most cases right in sight.

The effort to reclaim at-risk men that they may become productive and fit to become husbands and fathers is an extremely important factor in realigning and reviving marriage as the proper and right institution to raise children and develop productive families that serve God and minister to each other. Pastors, ministers, and even those who are not on the pastoral staff must support these initiatives or we will lose more men and more families. Our thinking about men at risk must be challenged. We must realize that many men who are thought to be deadbeats are men who find themselves overwhelmed and receive no positive feedback from their environment as to what resources are at their disposal to help make them productive. We must aggressively help them get back into the game. The longer we remain in our current mindset, the greater will grow the numbers of hopeless men.

Remember This:

Your perception of marriage and whom to marry can be a great issue and a hindrance to your marriage because some of what you learned about marriages while growing up may be wrong and destructive. Times are changing and the weapons and devices are more insidious. Following some simple guidelines about perception in marriage will help if you diligently apply these rules and seek God's face in prayer. More importantly, your views on marriage greatly affect the probability for success.

Remember that the marriage that is under your care is your marriage alone, and your parents' marriage should not be the model for your own unless it was one that fits into God's plan. Even then, God's plan only should be the model for your marriage.

Wives cannot expect their husbands to be like their fathers.

Husbands cannot expect their wives to be like their mothers.

As a wife, you are a grown woman who has the responsibility to take care of your husband as God directs and you agree. This doesn't mean being his mother; it means being a helper fit to complete his role as a man.

As a husband, you should love your wife as Christ loved the church and gave Himself up for it.

You may experience conflict in your marriage even if you are within the will of God.

Remain faithful to God's will for your marriage and He will lift you up.

If you are having trouble determining God's will, return to the Word and/or seek the counsel of the wise.

Remain in prayer.

CHAPTER TEN

Taking Your Marriage Out of Jeopardy and Keeping It Out

Fearing God and keeping His Commandments are a part of living that keeps marriages within the will of God.

Men:

1. Love your wife with all of your manhood.

Men, this means you must love your wives with all your might so that you may honor God because He provided woman that you may be whole as man. Besides, God said that husbands should love their wives as Christ loved the church and gave Himself up for it. And this is further reinforced by the Apostle Paul: "Husbands, love your wives [be affectionate and sympathetic with them] and do not be harsh or bitter or resentful toward them." **(Colossians 3:19)**

2. Speak to your wife the words of life and love.

A wise man once said of his wife: "Your stature is like that of the palm, and your breasts like clusters of fruit."

These are the words of Solomon. Sure, Solomon had many wives, but what is important here is the fact that his relationship with this wife is used as a model for how a man should speak to his wife. I have said something similar to this earlier, but it is so important to love your wives with your words that this concept must be repeated again even if you understood it the first time. The way God made woman demands that you love her with more than your labor and money even if some women only see love in terms of money and labor. Even if it is extremely hard to do, you must speak words of love to her because it releases into your home the Holy Spirit, which ministers' peace to your home that you may search out your love.

3. Get on your face before the Lord for your marriage.

This means pray with an earnestness that makes you completely submit to the will of God for your life and your marriage and the family that you and your wife create together and release into the world. If you have not given yourself completely to the Lord, this is where you begin. And since getting on your face before the Lord is where it all begins, if you like you may pray the following prayer, or if you want to pray your own prayer, get on your face and humble yourself and completely submit to His will:

Gracious, kind, loving, and all powerful heavenly Father in whom we live, move, and have our very being, great and unmatched is Your name above all names. Father, I know that it is Your will that we prosper and live according to Your plan. Father, I have sinned and I ask that You forgive me as I completely humble and submit myself, my marriage, and my flesh, spirit, and soul to Your will. I know that You created me alone and took my wife out of me and brought her to me because You love me and want to see my life filled with joy and love. For all these things You give me, my Father and my God, I thank you. I further ask You to come into my personal life and purify me. I believe that Jesus is the Christ and Son of God and I accept Him as my personal savior and invite Him to take over my life and marriage. Father, I thank You for just being You. Father, lead me and guide me and protect me in all that I do that I may please You. These wonderful blessings I ask and pray in Jesus' name, Amen.

4. Next, you must get your family into fellowship that you may continue your commitment to God by the submission of your marriage and family to Him. Once you do that, it is still not over. There are still things to monitor and adjustments to be made as you go.

5. Find out where you need help and get that help immediately.

6. Be Fruitful and multiply

I heard my pastor, Kirbyjon Caldwell of Windsor Village United Methodist Church, during our Sunday service explain that God spoke a single command to the cosmos. He said; "Be fruitful and multiply." Rev. Caldwell went on to explain that God commanded this also of mankind. Hearing this, it occurred to me that man has a need to be productive or he becomes dysfunctional. This is why hopelessness abounds when a man cannot find his way in this world. So if you find yourself unable to discover where you fit into God's plan to prosper, you should locate the resources to assist you in meeting your challenge to be productive and fruitful. The first place you should go is the church. You should challenge your local church to be more than an institution. It must also obey the command of God to be fruitful and multiply. The body of Christ is the place where you should be able to find out what God has for you in this life that you may be productive at a personal level and a blessing to your wife and family. Hopelessness is not of God; it is an instrument of Satan to ruin you and your family. I challenge you to seek God and challenge the church to assist you in finding your way back to productivity if this is your problem.

Seek Counsel Even If Nothing Seems Apparently Wrong

Remember that when God first created Adam and Eve and introduced them to each other, the first thing Satan did was to separate them from each other. Then he turned them against each other. Satan doesn't want two or more people to come together in God's plan, worshipping Him in spirit and truth with any part of their lives. Because man was not meant to be alone, God created fellowship with woman to fill this need. Because man and woman together were meant to be in fellowship, God places us with other believers that we may grow stronger in our faith. **Hebrews 10:24-26,** tells us the following:

And let us consider and give attentive, continuous care to watching over one another, studying how we may stir up [stimulate and incite] to love and helpful deeds and noble activities, Not forsaking or neglecting to assemble together [as believers], as is the habit of some people, but admonishing [warning, urging, and encouraging] one another, and all the more faithfully as you see the day approaching. For if we go on deliberately and willingly sinning after once acquiring the knowledge of the Truth, there is no longer any sacrifice left to atone for [our] sins [no further offering to which to look forward].

Fellowship is one element of Christian life that keeps families safe and keeps the counsel that couples receive pure and in line with God's plan. When we receive good, sound counsel, we tend to communicate more effectively, and the communication is much more useful when formulating solutions to our everyday problems. These days, advice comes from a vast array of resources and tends to become confusing because so many of these resources give advice that is contrary to what the Word tells us. This results in ineffective communication, which leads to confusion and failures at all levels and functions of marriage. It is important to qualify the sources of your advice and set a high standard for verifying it. Your marriage resources should come from the following sources in the order you will see below:

Your pastor or counselor directly attached to the church.

In most cases, if you have problems that require godly solutions, the first place you should go is to your pastor or minister whom you trust or with whom you have established a godly rapport. It is unfortunate that not all who profess to be ministers actually minister to the children of God. If you feel uncomfortable with your minister, seek out another minister whom you are sure is able to assist you to find God's blessing in your problem in the form of a godly solution. "The wise also will hear and increase in learning, and the person of understanding will acquire skill and attain to sound counsel [so that he may be able to steer his course rightly]." **(Proverbs 1:5, Amplified Bible)**

"Give instruction to a wise man and he will be yet wiser; teach a righteous man [one upright and in right standing with God] and he will increase in learning." **(Proverbs 9:9, Amplified Bible)**

2. Professional counseling.

Notice that the further away from the church we get in our resources, the more complicated it will be to determine if the advice is within the scope of the will of God. Many professional counselors will allow divorce to be an option. For Christian couples, divorce, even as a last option, is the worst thing to do. And in many cases instead of counseling the couple on how to have a better marriage, some professionals tend to focus on individual needs at the expense of the marriage. The more one focuses on themselves, the more separated and fractured the relationship grows and the more vulnerable to divorce the marriage becomes. Dr. Phil is not the answer, so stop taking his advice. What he says is not right for everyone. You must engage a solution and advice that is closer to your faith.

3. Seek advice from your immediate family: father, mother, grandmother, and grandfather.

Seeking advice from your family is a good idea if the advice you receive is within the will of God. But the pitfalls of seeking advice from family members include lack of discretion and in some cases, a tendency of parents and relatives to try to make your marriage too much like their own. And in some cases you may actually be the guilty party by trying to make your marriage like that of your parents or grandparents. When seeking and receiving advice from close relatives, remember that their marriage is their marriage alone, and it was entered into at a completely different time and place in society than was your marriage. Also remember that your marriage is your own, and it would be completely lazy to use your parent's marriage as a model for your own. It doesn't matter if your parent's marriage was or still is successful: your blessing is yours and so is your marriage. Your mother and father cannot bless your husband or wife for you in your marriage. This is exclusively your job.

Therefore a man shall leave his father and his mother and shall become united and cleave to his wife, and they shall become one flesh. And the man and his wife were both naked and were not embarrassed or ashamed in each other's presence. **(Genesis 2:24 -25)**

This passage illustrates that husband and wife are to be one, in a way that the two are completely vulnerable to each other spiritually as well as physically so that they may discern each other's needs, and their love will be manifested in actions that meet those needs just as God loves them and meets their needs each day. So when a spouse seeks advice, they should take care that the trust that comes from their mutual vulnerability is not defiled because some embarrassing details were revealed when it was best that they be left out unless the couple seeks advice together and agrees to reveal the sensitive details. And no matter how simple or sensitive the advice that is sought may be, the conversation should always end in a prayer that asks God to bless everyone with the wisdom and humility to serve and be an instrument of ministry.

4. Your Christian Friends.

Your brothers and sisters in Christ are also a great resource to utilize in protecting your marriage because many of us have the same struggles and trials and have mighty testimonies and experiences to share that may instantly bless your marriage with a piece of the puzzle that helps marriages to continue in their growth. Not only that, but so many of our brothers and sisters have a burden in their hearts to help someone to be blessed, and they are simply looking for an opportunity to be used by God to bless someone. And as with the advice you seek from your family, so should this conversation begin and end in prayer.

Notice that I did not advise you to look at television for advice on how to conduct your marriage. There is a reason for this and it may be obvious to some. For others it is important to understand that so much content is pushed through television that it becomes confusing and the messages are mixed in many cases; we are trying to avoid such confusion. Television should never be a source of counseling for your marriage.

Find Out If You Have Problems

Getting advice is good but it is also very important to make sure that you pay close attention to what is said and what is not said and that each major issue is brought into the light that it may be corrected and that you may be blessed. Three aspects of sin cause us to fail in everything, including marriage, and these include: lust of the flesh, lust of the eye, and the pride of life. We want material things, we love beautiful things, and we want to be powerful. Before I close our discussion, I want to discuss three major issues in marriages that cause their destruction. Money, communication (or a lack thereof), and too little or too much sex are the most misused elements of marriage.

Money

Money is important but it doesn't sustain life, only lifestyle.

Money problems get the blame as the primary cause of most marriage failures, but this is but a symptom of a deeper problem. The deeper problem is rooted in a quest for self-gratification from a source other than that which God intended. Reading the first Commandment gets us back on track. "You shall have no other gods before or besides Me." **(Exodus 20:3)** Notice that this is the very first Commandment. Interestingly, this suggests that people, though they know that God is Number One, tend to get their priorities out of order. These days, people worship their jobs, their possessions, and most of all they worship their money. A clear indicator of this fact is that most people spend more time chasing after money than they do ministering to their homes.

The more time you spend in a given area of life, the more you are dedicated to that place in life. But when you spend so much time working and chasing after money that the development of your family suffers, then you are placing your family at the terrible risk of complete destruction. The Bible mentions the proper ordering of priorities so many times that it becomes apparent that this is such a big problem that constant attention to being a good steward of what God has given you is of great importance. Since the first Commandment tells us to have no other gods before the Almighty, we must be careful and attentive that He remains our first priority. The Word tells us about money and the proper use of money and material items in your life. We read in the Books of Timothy and Hebrews the following:

Paul first warns us that the love of money is the root of all evil.

For the love of money is a root of all evils; it is through this craving that some have been led astray and have wandered from the faith and pierced themselves through with many acute [mental] pangs. **(1 Timothy 6:10)**

II. Secondly, we find in the following verse that selfishness and greed tend to go hand in hand to destroy the character of those who allow it.

For people will be lovers of self and [utterly] self-centered, lovers of money and aroused by an inordinate [greedy] desire for wealth, proud and arrogant and contemptuous boasters. They will be abusive [blasphemous, scoffing], disobedient to parents, ungrateful, unholy and profane. **(2 Timothy 3:2)**

III. In the Book of Hebrews we find agreement with the assertion that the character is soiled by a love of money that leads to further character denigration.

Let your character or moral disposition be free from love of money [including greed, avarice, lust, and craving for earthly possessions] and be satisfied with your present [circumstances and with what you have]; for He [God] Himself has said, I will not in any way fail you nor give you up nor leave you without support. [I will] not, [I will] not, [I will] not in any degree leave you helpless nor forsake nor let [you] down [relax My hold on you]! [Assuredly not!] **(Hebrews 13:5)**

To be free of these traps, you must do several things:

Pray for direction and understanding of finances and wisdom in the use and care of your finances in your marriage. This is the first step: completely submit your finances to God that He may bless you and protect you from temptation and inspire you to seek sound assistance to solidify your financial situation.

Openly and freely discuss and reveal all financial issues between the marriage partners because there are no longer individual finances. Remember, you have a marriage. This is a state of oneness between two people to love each other, meet mutual needs, and worship God together. If either of you have had challenges in the past or currently have financial challenges, you must disclose these items because to overcome these challenges and be delivered, everyone must know the situation. You may first pray, then plan, and finally execute your plan for deliverance from the financial challenges you both have.

3. Take active control of all financial transactions and activities. Every day you must make a conscious effort to take control over your behavior by remaining in prayer and doing what you know is right for your finances in the marriage. This may mean less eating out or a few less pairs of shoes or maybe a smaller house or a more practical car. This could also mean that you must simply be patient and let God bless you in His time. Patience in financial challenges is most difficult to have because these challenges cause people to react in anger and even rage. Again, pray about the decisions you make every day, and make the right choices. It is just as easy to live within your means, as it is to overextend yourself financially. The key to developing good financial habits is to begin sound practices and keep them in place. If you need help in conducting your daily financial behavior, you have a spouse who may be inspirational in helping you and may even suggest that you both get some professional help to get back on track.

4. Remain focused on keeping your finances under your complete control. Develop a plan and remain faithful in both prayer and execution.

5. Organize your bank accounts. Couples before they marry in many cases have bank accounts but some do not because living paycheck to paycheck, on a very tight budget, makes it a great challenge to maintain a bank account, but with diligence this challenge can be overcome and you can receive deliverance. Organizing your bank accounts (for those who have them) is an important tactic in the strategy for overcoming bondage to your finances.

You must consolidate all of your finances into only two accounts. One joint checking account and one joint savings account are sufficient to take care of your financial needs. This eliminates the secrets that begin to bite away at the fabric of honesty in your marriage. Once you complete this point of organization, you must put all of your money into these accounts without holding out. Remember Ananias and Saphira? You may not be stricken by sudden death, but Satan wants you to think that nondisclosure and dishonesty in your finances can be an advantage to you—but it won't. Eventually, there will be many small deaths in your marriage that may result in its destruction if you fail to be completely honest and open about money.

Failure to disclose blind spots in marriages can cause serious problems should some circumstance arise that demands emergency action. If everyone is not aware of what is going on, then no one has a full picture of how to deal with the issue. In almost every case, the partner who does not know of the issue or doesn't know enough about the issue has some God-given strength to contribute that might deliver you from the snare. God trusted you with His Child, and in the matter of finances you must live worthy of His trust. You must honor His trust. Simply put, you can't have secret stashes of money here and there in bank accounts or credit unions or financial investments. Don't correct any failures to disclose and see what happens to your spouse's trust. Keep that from happening, and let God bless your finances.

6. Save your money.

Being conservative with your money is critical in making sure that there is no lack when the time for tapping into your cash reserves is at hand. But you must be wise and of a single mind about how you will conduct the saving of money. As with any financial decision, this one also requires a plan as well as complete and faithful execution. In more and more cases savings plans and investment activities need professional assistance to get started and to maintain unless you and your spouse have the skill to manage them. Make sure that even if you decide together to manage your savings and investments, you get some professional advice to validate that your decisions are sound. And in any case and for any plan or decision, remain faithful in prayer.

7. Overcome your emotional attachment to money.

This is one of the most important tasks in life as it relates to your physical existence. Money has its place, but money is to be placed into where it belongs in terms of all that God has given you stewardship over. Money is a resource that, if used wisely, conserved, given freely as required, and its importance held in proper perspective, you will find to be a powerful servant. Money is here to serve you. That is why your money is imprinted with the words "In God We Trust"; money will serve its master.

The question is, Are you the master and steward of your money or have you allowed your humanity and spirit to be inappropriately tied to money, making it the master without regard to anything living or dead? There are many things you may remember about money, but if you remember to place God first, your perspective about money will allow your spirit to be delivered from the stresses associated with a lack of money or an inappropriate faith in money.

What you should remember above all is that if you want for something, you must do two things faithfully. The first is to wait upon (serve) the Lord, and secondly, when you get money, be it a small amount or a great windfall, you must serve God by the way you manage this blessing from Him. This means a married couple must work together to make God's blessings a constant reality in their lives. When we fail to do that, God's blessings become less real, more distant to us, and seem intended for someone else instead of being our right as an heir of God. You will become delivered from an emotional attachment to money by understanding who you are and what the promises of God are because of your identity in Christ. **(Romans 8:17; Genesis 12:1-2)** When you understand your identity in Christ, you will begin to understand that it is not how many hours you work and how much money you make, but how you work and how you manage and care for what God has given you as His heir.

Communication

If your spouse doesn't know about something or understand your feelings, it just may be because you didn't tell them. Communication transactions are complete when a message is sent, perceived by the audience, and the audience replies or transmits feedback. But problems can happen between two communicators. At times problems in communication are a symptom of a larger, more insidious issue, but that aside, being delivered from communication issues takes more work than most people are willing to put in. Today's society demands that we reach instant solutions or face the disposal of relationships. Here are some simple steps to isolate and gain control of communication issues by being deliberate and prayerful before, during, and after you have had the discussion.

Pray before you talk.

Look your partner in the eye when you are talking to him or her.

Look your partner in the eye when he or she is talking to you.

Repeat back what you think your partner said so they may know that you received the message.

Take your time and shape your words to give life to your spouse.

Begin developing solutions to the problem during the conversation even if it is only a single-action item.

Pray to God for deliverance and clarity.

If you find yourself languishing in repeated arguments that almost never end in resolution, it's time for professional help. Don't wait until it's too late to get help. If you want your marriage to work, God has given you a spirit that will cry out to Him, and He will answer your cries and send you the help you need. You must also put your mind in a place where He may reach you. Remaining within the will of God will require that you choose to serve Him faithfully. Your choices make a huge difference as to when you receive your deliverance.

Sex

"And if *you* don't make him feel like a man *who is*? ...a man *cheats* because he ain't getting what he needs at home, emotionally, spiritually, physically..." (Dr. Juanita Bynum-Weeks, sermon, 2002, Pride Versus the Proverbs 31 Woman)

Now it's time to get real. Sex is not a problem in marriages. Sex has never caused a marriage to break up nor has it caused marriages to remain whole. So if anyone spends a lot of time talking about sexuality or sex and blaming sex or sexuality for problems in marriages, they are completely incorrect and have misplaced blame for marital problems just as if they had misappropriated funds over which they were given charge. They failed to correctly assign blame to the real culprit for the failure of marriages. Sexuality is a very important part of a marriage, but this aspect of the marriage relationship is shaped and formed long before the two become one.

A childhood that saw a mother physically, sexually, or verbally abused could contribute to the development of an adult who clings to so many misconceptions about sexuality that these toxic elements of early childhood development have misshapen his or her perceptions and the way she or he processes the elements of intimacy. Such individuals are likely to attach themselves to someone with whom it is not healthy to share their spirit. Many of these same people are in the church. In fact, I would venture to assert that *most* of these individuals are in the church.

So the problem of sexuality in relationships is rooted in what children are taught about how boys and girls, who grow up to be men and women, should treat each other in their relationships. If all that a boy or girl sees from their parents' relationship are disconnection, neglect, and violence, they will not be able to learn how to establish intimacy and spiritual connections, and they may have significant challenges with intimate relationships as adults. Many of us come from such homes, and as a result, we experience challenges that in many cases we cannot overcome without help. The question is, If there are sexual problems in a marriage, how do you overcome the challenges that arise from this issue?

First, one must be honest about their strengths and weaknesses in the area of sexual intimacy. Second, the issues must be addressed prayerfully, aggressively, and directly, and if professional help is required to overcome the challenge, get it as soon as you know the problem requires that assistance. Even if you don't think you need professional assistance with your sex life in the marriage, at least speak with your pastor or minister and find out if there are resources in your local congregation. If resources aren't available to you in your local church, challenge your church and everyone in your local fellowship to assist you in locating or providing the resources you need to develop into a healthy child of God. If you find that you do not have significant problems in your sex life but you want to become closer as a couple, hopefully you will find help here. Another important point that I cannot stress enough is that sex in itself is not intimacy. Intimacy must be established independently of any physical act. Intimacy comes from your ministry to any person you love.

Getting Down to Business

In this day and age we find that too many people are looking for quick fixes to the challenges they are faced with day to day without being realistic enough to realize that the problems didn't just show up one day or even over a period of months but were developed and socialized and learned over years. The first thing a married couple needs to do is to get to know each other intimately. This means finding in your spouse what God shows you every day, that is, things you are compelled to love about your spouse. Find out what made your spirits come together. You can do this by simply learning to talk to each other about things other than work and the daily routine. Nothing can make a marriage fall into neglect and disrepair faster than always and every day, day in and day out, talking about your jobs.

Find each other in your conversation. God made woman for man, and in the Garden of Eden there was so much wonder because the world was new and there were fewer distractions. Now there are so many distractions that couples lose each other in fouled up priorities of life. So to begin your own marriage revival, you must re-tool your mutual conversation. The question is, Where do we begin? Since we find that for every aspect of life the Word has an example, we can go back to the Word for the answer.

It's hard to know where to begin with the issue of sex when it comes to talking about things that can be issues because life is so complicated and the issues are so diverse. But the place to start, as I see it, is with the fact that marriages begin with two people who have decided to love each other in spite of their baggage. But is this really true? Is it that we come together in marriage for comfort and companionship? Or do we settle for the one we think is safe and can make us some money and buy us things? Are we capable of placing our spiritual security in a relationship like that? Or do we place our spiritual security in material things and attach our sexuality to material accomplishment? Is it that we play this trick / hooker game and trade sexual favors for security? Are women really selling their bodies for security when they get married? Are men really deciding to buy the best woman they can find to meet their physical needs? What's for sale? Who is for sale? Who is buying? I ask these questions to get to the point of the lives of many so-called Christians. Many Christians live their love lives in this way.

The true point is that God made us one way but people often decide to misplace spiritual trust into things that rust, corrode, and pass away instead of worshipping God and allowing Him to sustain our spiritual lives. You sex life begins with your right-living spirit, soul, and body. You must understand that your behavior exposes your spirit, soul, and body to elements that can edify the whole, cause your whole being to settle into a condition of stasis or stagnation, or cause the death of your persona, be it slowly or instantaneously. What you have been exposed to in your past directly affects your perception of marriage and the way you minister to your mate. You may be completely giving and totally committed to your mate. You may be pensive, tentative, or timid, waiting for a reason to surrender to meeting the needs of your mate. You may be completely dead spiritually and have disconnected from the mechanisms God has placed inside of you to complete the model of mankind God created in the beginning. Your nature, without being touched by outside worldly forces, places man and woman together in a holy and sacred union anointed by God that you may come together to appreciate the wonders of God in unconditional mutual love as you worship Him in spirit and truth.

To begin with, we must take for granted that when people get married they have come from two separate and different places with two separate pasts. The central problem is that the two people come together for one purpose with two parts. You come together in love to first worship God, and secondly to love (minister to) each other. With this in mind, the first thing you must do together after you take your vows in public is to make a covenant with God and with each other personally and privately. You must totally surrender to God's will for marriage in your lives because now—no matter what your past may be—you have become one person, and your whole lives must now show that commitment. Your bodies are no longer your personal property; they now belong as much to your spouse as to yourself.

You must now minister faithfully to your spouse. Sex is the physical ministry that pours two souls together in love before God who continually blesses that union as long as you are faithful and surrender to His will for your marriage. Before we go on, I must explain that sex is a spiritual union of two human spirits that begins with physical touch and was created by God for men and women who are married to each other. This physical union begins with complete commitment and complete surrender to God's will, for this is the first human union He created. When God touched Adam, He took from him a rib, created Eve, and introduced her to him. So from His touch alone God connected with Adam, taking a piece of him, and out of that touch He then completed mankind with the creation and introduction of Eve to Adam.

Adam's response to this was immediate and showed that God's touch created life and completion for mankind. So with this example in mind, we must know that in marriage every time we touch each other and show affection we are renewing life and continually completing and affirming each other. Affectionate touching between spouses connects our spirits and continually gives life to a marriage relationship. A marriage without the spiritual connection of sex combined with affectionate touching would not be able to survive because we were created to love each other this way. So when husbands and wives touch in any way, be it sexual or not, this is a method of continuous affirmation and renewal.

Touch is a powerful agent of life! Studies show that infants exposed to invasive surgical procedures and traumatic medical experiences that cause pain respond remarkably well to this simple and overlooked method of ministry. Babies were monitored and were found to have longer periods of deeper sleep and healed much faster. The overall result of this treatment resulted in lower stress levels and happier babies. NICU nurse Annette Reed began this kind of treatment at Vanderbilt University Medical Center.

Reed recalls a particular patient whom she began working with halfway through a six-month admission. The baby's mother was unable to visit the hospital regularly. Along with her fragile medical condition, this unhappy infant had developed severe touch aversion. Reed helped create a strong team of nurses for daily massage therapy. "By the time she left, she was a happy, smiling baby. I know that we made a tremendous difference in her life," Reed said. "We are constantly looking for ways to improve care in the NICU, and this is one more way nurses can make a difference in patients' lives."

If this therapy works so well for babies, how much more effective can we be as husbands and wives, as instruments of God in the daily ministry to our mates of simple, loving touch? We don't have to wait until our mates are ill to renew them and minister to them so that they may know God loves them through their spouse's touch. Touching your spouse is a ministry. As we go through life, men and women deal with life in different ways and react in different ways to the stresses of life. As I illustrated earlier, men are expressions of God's power, and since this is true, God gave man dominion over the land, sky, and sea. Because of this dominion, men constantly need reminders that God gave them charge over His creation and thereby reaffirmed man's power.

Man must then take excellent care of all that God has given him as a part of his worship of God to show his reverence, respect, and gratitude to God. So when men look at the beauty of the whole creation and see the entire splendor of God, they can turn their attention to their wives and begin to truly

116

appreciate all that God is blessing them with through their wives. At this point, the natural tendency for man is to draw physically near to his wife unless Satan is causing him to act unnaturally. When man draws near to his wife in a physical union, he is blessed with the physical sensation of love that God has provided him with so that he may totally focus on God with his wife. Thus the creation is complete, and man worships God, and God continues to love man and woman as He did in the beginning. Nothing should come between the love of a husband and wife because this is the first relationship that God created between two people. From this relationship, children learn how to form and maintain their own relationships.

Sex does not begin with intercourse; it begins with touch, and this touch escalates into the explosive joy of lovemaking. Touching and being in touch are very similar, but they are very different. Touching is the beginning of being in touch with your mate. It is the beginning of finding his or her spirit and ministering to it so that you may grow closer and understand what God is telling you about how your spirits function and how your spirits interact with His spirit in worship. He gave you to each other, so you must search each other out before anything else so that your home is strong and that nothing can challenge your marriage. Here are some important aspects of touch that may help you to become close to your spouse sexually and spiritually.

When you touch your mate, she or he actually feels you unless you withhold your spirit from them.

You should never withhold your spirit from your mate.

You should never withhold sex from your mate under reasonable circumstances. In case of illness, you should see to it that your mate's health needs are attended to so that you may come together sexually without harming either or both of you. This is without exception. In **I Corinthians 7:3-10,** the Amplified translation tells us:

The husband should give to his wife her conjugal rights [goodwill, kindness, and what is due her as his wife], and likewise the wife to her husband.

For the wife does not have [exclusive] authority and control over her own body, but the husband [has his rights]; likewise also the husband does not have [exclusive] authority and control over his body, but the wife [has her rights].

Do not refuse and deprive and defraud each other [of your due marital rights], except perhaps by mutual consent for a time, so that you may devote yourselves unhindered to prayer. But afterward resume marital relations, lest Satan tempt you [to sin] through your lack of restraint of sexual desire.

The passage goes on to admonish married couples in the Lord to refrain from separating from each other:

But to the unmarried people and to the widows, I declare that it is well [good, advantageous, expedient, and wholesome] for them to remain [single] even as I do.

But if they have not self-control [restraint of their passions], they should marry. For it is better to marry than to be aflame [with passion and tortured continually with ungratified desire].

But to the married people I give charge—not I but the Lord—
that the wife is not to separate from her husband.

In this passage Paul makes a distinction between
married and unmarried, telling the single ones in Christ that if
they are tempted too greatly by their natural attraction and
compulsion for sex, then they should marry that they may enjoy
this relationship and not be in a state of torment and torture or
sin for having sex outside of marriage. It is important to note
also that abstinence is only for those who are not married. If a
husband or wife refuses their mate, they place their spouse in
a state of continual need. If this need for contact continues
unmet, the result will be a state of continual torment from
ungratified desire because one partner is refusing the other for
whatever reason. Paul mentions that the Lord commands
husbands and wives to not refuse each other the physical
ministry of sex. Based on this fact, if one refuses their spouse
sexual intimacy, they sin themselves and actually put their
spouse in danger of committing sin. Remember that the
Lord Himself told us that if we love Him, we would keep his
Commandments.

Remember This:

You don't have to have a problem to seek counsel.
Seeking counsel before a problem arises may keep it from
becoming an issue in the first place. Make absolutely sure that
you pay attention to every aspect of your marriage. Any area
that you neglect may cause terrible conflict. Be ever on guard.
The enemy is lurking.

CHAPTER ELEVEN

Keeping Faithfully the Covenant

You often here the statement made: "You made your bed. Now lie in it!" Too many times this is the statement forced upon those who have premarital sex that results in a pregnancy, but this adage also applies completely to those who are married and think that it is within their right to refuse their husbands or wives. You made a covenant before God and man that you would be responsible and love your mate under all conditions. So grow up and keep your word faithfully. Life is not for the faint of heart. Your commitment to God is most important, and how you respond to your mate is key to how you will be blessed. Complete submission to the will of God in your marriage will redeem and revive your marriage. Your faithfulness and total willingness to minister to God's gift to you will be a source of renewal in your marriage. Wait upon your mate. This means to serve him or her, and your strength will be renewed. Wait upon them as if your life depended upon it, and you are sure to be renewed. Here is the confirmation of what I tell you: "But they that wait upon the Lord shall renew their strength; they shall mount up with wings as eagles; they shall run, and not be weary; and they shall walk, and not faint." **Isaiah 40:31**

Let's divide the scripture into two parts much like a logical argument, an "if then" statement if you will. The scripture says "they," meaning all who wait upon the Lord. Taken into this part we see that the scripture speaks of a group of people indicated by the word "they." So we can assume it means everyone. Subdividing the first part into two parts, we find what is left of the first part is: "that wait upon the Lord." This is the part that many people simply fail to understand because of the archaic use of the phrase "wait upon." In many cases you hear people say, "What are you waiting on?" This is a misuse of the phrase "waiting on" because in this context the language implies that you are actually waiting for someone something or some event to happen. In the context of the scripture "wait upon" means "to serve." This is indicated by the historical reference that faithfulness is applied to service to God. God told Abraham in **Genesis 12: 1-3:**

Now [in Haran] the Lord said to Abraham, Go for yourself [for your own advantage] away from your country, from your relatives and your father's house, to the land that I will show you.

And I will make of you a great nation, and I will bless you [with abundant increase of favors] and make your name famous and distinguished, and you will be a blessing [dispensing good to others].

And I will bless those who bless you [who confer prosperity or happiness upon you] and curse him who curses or uses insolent language toward you; in you will all the families and kindred of the earth be blessed [and by you they will bless themselves].

Here it is established that if Abraham does what God asks, He would bless Abraham. So to be blessed, Abraham needed to act on his faith actively instead of waiting for something to happen. He had to act to get God's blessing.

This is the structure of a covenant. You will see throughout the Bible that covenants were established by God, commanding the subject to act in order to receive God's blessing. The same applies in **Isaiah 40:31.** The scripture so far reads: "But everyone who serves the Lord..."

Let us now analyze the second half of the covenant. We find that God does something wondrous when we need it most. He renews us. He allows us to fly with wings as eagles, and run and not be weary, and walk and not faint under the heat of our challenges. The prophet wasn't just making a passive statement; he was reinforcing and restating a covenant with God's people. You don't sit and wait for something to happen; you act and serve God in faith, and He will find what you need and give it to you as He always has throughout time, as He does now, and as He ever shall. God bless you all.

A Final Word

It is my prayer that we have covered enough material in a way that will cause you to seek the face of God in your marriage. The result of seeking God's will for your lives in marriage will be the crushing of curses that have been passed on from generation to generation, ruining perfectly good homes and laying marriages to waste and leaving people in ruin. Your marriage can be the place where God blesses you, and all who are in fellowship with you will know from your example that God is on the throne, and through that knowledge they can come to the Lord and submit their marriages to Him that they may be blessed through all eternity.

Living right takes a little effort and commitment on your part every day. And for each day you follow Jesus, you will be renewed and strengthened so that your journey will be in the will of God. But you must trust Him and submit completely to Him. He has a plan for you. Find out more about His plan for your life and abide in it.

NOTES

NOTES

NOTES

NOTES

NOTES

NOTES

NOTES

NOTES

NOTES